Jessica Swale

Jessica Swale is an Olivier Award-winning playwright, screenwriter and director. She trained at the Royal Central School of Speech and Drama and the University of Exeter.

Her plays include *Nell Gwynn*, which transferred to London's West End, starring Gemma Arterton, and won the 2016 Olivier Award for Best New Comedy, *Blue Stockings*, now a set text on the GCSE Drama syllabus, and *Thomas Tallis* (all for Shakespeare's Globe); *All's Will That Ends Will* (Bremer Shakespeare Company); adaptations of *The Jungle Book* (Northampton); *Far from the Madding Crowd*, *Sense and Sensibility* (Watermill Theatre); *The Secret Garden*, *Stig of the Dump* (Grosvenor Park); radio play *Love* [*sic*] for BBC Radio 4, and *The Mission*, about illegal adoptions in the 1920s (for Chichester Festival Theatre).

Jessica set up Red Handed Theatre Company in 2005, to develop new plays and revive classics. As Artistic Director, productions included *The Rivals* starring Celia Imrie, and the first major revival of Hannah Cowley's *The Belle's Stratagem*, which won her a nomination for Best Director at the Evening Standard Awards. Red Handed won Best Ensemble at the Peter Brook Empty Space Awards 2012.

Other productions include *Bedlam* (Shakespeare's Globe); *Sleuth* (Watermill); *Fallen Angels* (Salisbury Playhouse); *Winter* (TNL, Canada); *The Busy Body*, *Someone to Watch Over Me* (Southwark) and *The School for Scandal* (Park Theatre). Jessica was Associate Director to Max Stafford-Clark at Out of Joint from 2007–2010, and directs at drama schools including RADA, LAMDA and Guildhall.

Jessica is an Associate Artist with Youth Bridge Global, an international NGO which uses theatre as a tool for promoting social change in war-torn and developing nations.

As such, she has lived in the Marshall Islands and in Bosnia and Herzegovina, directing Shakespeare productions including *The Comedy of Errors*, *Much Ado About Nothing*, *Twelfth Night* and *The Tempest*.

As screenwriter, Jessica is currently writing *Nell Gwynn* (Working Title), *Longbourn* (Studio Canal), *The Horrible Histories Movie* (Altitude), and is directing her first feature film, *Summerland*, for Shoe Box Pictures. She has written three titles in Nick Hern Books' popular *Drama Games* series: *for Classrooms and Workshops*, *for Devising*, and *for Rehearsals*.

Lois Jeary

Lois was assistant director on the RADA production of *Blue Stockings* in 2012 and subsequently assisted Jessica Swale on *The School for Scandal* (Park Theatre and Theatre Royal, Bury St Edmunds) and *The Rover* (RADA). She has directed new writing at Tristan Bates Theatre and the RADA Festival, and written on theatre for *Exeunt* and *A Younger Theatre*, as well as having work published in the *Guardian*. Lois holds a degree in Government from the London School of Economics and Political Science, and an MA in Text and Performance from RADA and Birkbeck, University of London.

JESSICA SWALE'S
Blue Stockings

A Guide for Studying and Staging the Play

Jessica Swale and Lois Jeary

NICK HERN BOOKS

London

www.nickhernbooks.co.uk

A Nick Hern Book

Jessica Swale's Blue Stockings – Page to Stage
first published in Great Britain in 2017
as a paperback original by Nick Hern Books Limited,
The Glasshouse, 49a Goldhawk Road, London W12 8QP

Jessica Swale's Blue Stockings – Page to Stage
copyright © 2017 Jessica Swale and Lois Jeary

Page to Stage series
copyright © 2017 Nick Hern Books Limited

Jessica Swale and Lois Jeary have asserted their right to be
identified as the authors of this work

Cover photograph © Manuel Harlan: Ellie Piercy and
Olivia Ross in the 2013 production at Shakespeare's Globe

Designed and typeset by Nick Hern Books, London
Printed in the UK by CPI Group (UK) Ltd

A CIP catalogue record for this book is available
from the British Library

ISBN 978 1 84842 623 8

Contents

Introduction

ORIGINS

I never intended to write *Blue Stockings*. In fact, I never planned to be a writer at all. I thought that writers were middle-aged men with writing sheds and long beards. I live on a second floor, so have no shed, and thankfully no sign of a beard. But then something unexpected happened; I came across a nugget of history, an untold moment from the past, and that changed everything. I hadn't been looking for a story, but one seemed to find me.

I was working as a theatre director with Max Stafford-Clark at Out of Joint, and was busy doing research for another play set in the 1800s. I was trying to work out what life was like for young Victorian women – what were their prospects, their hopes, their ambitions? In doing so, I stumbled upon the fact that most universities in England didn't allow female students until the twentieth century. And, even worse, those that did tended to make life *very* difficult for those girls.

If you were a young woman at university in the late 1800s, your day might look something like this: you would walk a very long way from your out-of-town college to lectures, where you'd be mocked by both students and teachers, be forced to sit at the back, and have your work left unmarked or rejected. You would often be denied entry to your lectures because tutors would deem you a distraction or unworthy of their time. You would be humiliated in the street. And what's more, because universities weren't set up to accommodate women, you would have had great trouble going about your daily business. There were no toilets for women, so you may have had to carry a chamber pot with you, and hope to use it in a quiet street without being spotted. You may have been banned from the canteen in case you distracted the men on their lunch break. And what's worse, you'd be told by all and sundry that you were unnatural – an oddity. You would be treated as an outcast. Men don't want to marry 'academic' women, they want quiet wives who will be obedient spouses and good mothers. Who wants a wife with aspirations?! God forbid!

In the 1800s, most people (women included) fervently believed that a woman's place was in the home. To be a nice, demure wife, who provided dinner and raised children, was the standard. Woe betide the woman who dared to have an opinion, let alone wanted a job! The idea that women might attempt to be more like men by pursuing careers was seen as the beginning of the end of society.

There was an overwhelming belief that women should not enter higher education. Many women didn't go to secondary school, and those that did learned only the feminine arts, like needlework and flower arranging. Women didn't need to learn; they just needed to behave. Therefore, most universities kept their doors firmly closed to women, regardless of how brilliant their minds were.

Reading about this – a subject on which I knew nothing – shocked me profoundly. I might have believed it, had it been hundreds of years ago, but this wasn't the experience of women in ancient societies. It was little more than a century ago. My grandmother was born in the following decade. And this was happening *in England*. It felt very close to home.

I count my own university years as some of my happiest and most rewarding. It was a time when I was allowed the opportunity to grow up, flex my mental muscles and discover who I might go on to be. The idea that society would be appalled by women like me and my friends, who simply wanted to study, seemed outrageous. At first it made me angry; then it made me think; then, crucially, it made me want to speak. To talk about this injustice. To tell everyone that it happened. That here, in Britain, there was a time when women weren't allowed to think and learn, and had to fight for their right to an education. To remind us how lucky we are to have access to learning, when so many women in the world don't. In developing countries, as I write, one in two girls don't have access to secondary education. Many have no access to education at any level. Today. The greatest way to empower people is to give them knowledge – to educate people so they can help themselves. Education is important and it is a right. It's there in the Geneva Convention, alongside the right to freedom and the right to life. I wanted to write about that.

So there I was. With a subject I felt passionate about that needed a platform. And how could I make that happen? Simple. I worked in the theatre; it had to be a play.

The idea of making the play, however, was daunting. Creating a play is a huge task, and whilst I had directed many, I'd never written one. I needed to find a writer, who could write the script, which I would direct. But then I began imagining. I started to imagine a girl getting off the train, her dainty shoes a stark contrast to the crowd of men's feet on the platform. I started imagining the girl who has to retake the year because her nerves get the better of her. The boy who meets the girl... the brave teachers and their sacrifices... the funny lessons on bikes...

And that was it. I couldn't possibly hand it over to someone else. I had gone too far. I had to write it. And that was the beginning of *Blue Stockings*.

And when I wasn't sure where to start, I returned to the research. I looked at pictures. I delved into the archives at Girton College. Wading through their stacks, I came across portraits, photographs of lectures and images of old Cambridge. But there was one single picture I couldn't take my eyes off – an image that became the touchstone of the play and gave me motivation to write every time I lost my nerve.

It was a small photograph, taken in 1897, blurred and in black and white. In it, a mannequin is hoisted high on ropes above a street packed with men in boater hats. The mannequin is a girl on a bike, wearing blue stockings (a symbol of academic women). She's strung up, helpless, a grim mockery of university women. Underneath her, the crowd are protesting. Nearby, students are throwing rocks and pulling down theatre hoardings. And, shortly after the picture was taken, the mannequin was paraded through the streets and set on fire, like Guy Fawkes, whilst onlookers whooped and cheered as the effigy of a young woman was burned in the heart of the city. And why? Because women had had the audacity to ask for the right to graduate. Asked to be recognised for work they had done. Having studied for three years, on identical courses to the men, all they wanted was for their qualifications to be recognised. And they were denied.

The emotions present in that moment. The fear that makes people burn effigies. The certainty with which the university campaigned to keep women out. The fact that men returned in their hundreds to vote against the women. And yet, in the face of this hatred and injustice, those girls sacrificed everything to stay. And they couldn't have done it without brave teachers, often men, who put their own careers on the line to stand by their female students.

This was a time of turbulence and social change on a far wider scale. Industrialisation had swept the nation and changed the face of our towns and cities. We were on the verge of the Boer War, and the suffrage movement was beginning to spread. Change induces fear, and for many, women's will to challenge the status quo was the tip of a much more dangerous iceberg in which England, as they knew it, was on the brink of irreversible change. If women weren't content to stay at home as housewives, what would happen to the country? Who would nurture the children? What would become of the family? The nation? It would be a disaster.

Blue Stockings is a fictional story, inspired by real events. It tells the story of a group of extraordinary girls in their first year at Cambridge. The year is 1896. The girls were expected to develop into polite young ladies, with harmless hobbies like embroidery and flower arranging, before settling down to married lives. But was that enough for them? Absolutely not.

They were women who wanted more. Who wanted experiences outside the world they were born in to. Women who I wanted to write about and who deserve to be remembered. Women who wanted to *know*. To understand the properties of light. To translate Virgil. To cure diseases, to invent, to comprehend the boundaries of space. They wanted to learn. And they would do anything for the chance to do so.

Blue Stockings is the story of those girls.

I wanted to call it *Blue Stockings* because the term tells us something of the perception of educated women over time. 'Bluestocking' was originally coined in the 1700s to describe clever women who met at literary salons to discuss intellectual ideas. Thus, to be a member of a Blue Stockings society was desirable and a privilege; to have knowledge and to be a little learned was seen as a classy pursuit. But, over time, it became a derogatory phrase used to poke fun at women who were perceived to be scholarly oddities – women who didn't match the feminine ideal. So I wanted to reclaim the term.

Blue Stockings is two words as it is a deliberate reference to the clothing: in the play, the boys buy blue stockings to put on the effigy. Stockings are also a symbol of sex and female sexuality. It's a bit cheeky. As the then Artistic Director of Shakespeare's Globe, Dominic Dromgoole, said to me, 'Good title, *Blue Stockings*. The women'll come cos they'll think it's feminist; the men'll come cos they'll think it's sexy.'

Some of you reading this book will likely be staging your own productions of *Blue Stockings*. I hope you enjoy this text as a helpful and inspiring resource. Compiled with my assistant director Lois Jeary, a formidable mind and a first-class researcher, this guide aims to take you through the process of staging the play, to consider each of the elements of production, from sound and music to design and rehearsals. You'll also find notes from our rehearsal process, extracts from my working diaries, notes and exercises, ideas for you to try, and contextual research to immerse you and your company in the world of the play.

'Let the petticoats descend!'

Jessica Swale

The playtext of *Blue Stockings* by Jessica Swale is published by Nick Hern Books (revised edition, 2014, ISBN 978 1 84842 329 9), and can be purchased with a discount from www.nickhernbooks.co.uk. All page references in this book are to this edition.

Cambridge on the day of the vote, 1897. Courtesy of the Mistress and Fellows, Girton College, Cambridge.

Blue Stockings
In Rehearsal

The World of the Play

Blue Stockings is set in 1896–7 – a time when Queen Victoria was on the throne, the colonies of the British Empire spread from Newfoundland in the northern hemisphere to New Zealand in the southern, and only men who owned or rented property above a certain value had the right to vote.

In terms of both the law and the way society viewed them, Victorian women were second-class citizens; so the women in this play have a great deal to fight against, if their aim is to be taken seriously as intelligent citizens who might like the chance to work.

Understanding the historical context is crucial to telling the story of the play. Although the play is firmly set in Victorian England, there is a contrast between the expectations this sets up and the way its female characters behave. They are not your typical Victorians, and therein lies the drama. They are women who defy the conventions of their time; Jessica says the characters are 'bursting out of their corsets – trying to move forward before their peers have caught up. It is important that, whilst they inhabit a Victorian world, the women's energies and sensibilities are ahead of their time. That's where the interesting juxtaposition lies.'

The actor, director or designer's primary task is to interpret and bring to life the characters and text. *Blue Stockings* features both real and fictional characters and incidents, so thoughtfully applied research can illuminate those interpretations. Everyone uses research in different ways and, although some might do it purely for their own information, establishing ways to share findings amongst a cast ensures that everyone works from the same starting point.

In rehearsals, Jessica often gives each cast member a particular topic to research and then asks them to present their findings to the rest of the company, so that all can share in building the world of the play. It is important that actors choose a topic that relates to their character so that the research is useful rather than simply academic. Jessica also encourages actors to find a playful, fun, inventive way of sharing their findings, rather than simply giving a talk full of dry information. They may present it in an exercise, as a playlet or as a chat show. When rehearsing Hannah Cowley's eighteenth-century comedy of manners *The Belle's Strata-gem*, they even had one research session that spoofed an episode of *Made in Chelsea*! The more palatable and active the information becomes, the more it will go in.

Here is a list of suggested research topics, followed by an introduction to some key themes:

- The history of Girton College – including Elizabeth Welsh and her predecessor, Emily Davies.
- The daily routine at Girton.
- The riot and the vote on women's graduation rights.
- The role of a university lecturer at Cambridge.
- What courses consisted of at Cambridge.
- What social lives were like in Cambridge.
- The geography of Cambridge – the town, the locations in the play, and what there was to do.
- Social class at Cambridge and beyond.
- Famous Cambridge students and their experiences.
- The science of the play, and astronomy in particular.
- Hysteria – the study of it and what people believed about it.
- Relationships – marriage, courting and expectations.
- Suffrage.
- Politics of the 1890s.
- Arts of the 1890s.

THE RIGHTS OF WOMEN IN
NINETEENTH–CENTURY ENGLAND

'Under exclusively man-made laws women have been reduced to the most abject condition of legal slavery in which it is possible for human beings to be held.'[1]

Florence Fenwick Miller,
in a speech at the National Liberal Club, 1890

The women in *Blue Stockings* defy society's expectations of them. In order to communicate this spirit and zeal, actors need to have an understanding of what those historical constraints were. It is also helpful to appreciate that the play is set in a time when the position of women in society was starting to shift and campaigns for women's rights were gathering momentum.

The nineteenth century was a time of division between the sexes that crystallised in the doctrine of men and women occupying separate spheres. The man's role was considered to be engaging in public and economic life – going out to work, being the wage earner and representing the family in matters of law or politics. Meanwhile, the woman's place was in the home with all its attendant domestic responsibilities, such as cooking, needlework and, perhaps most importantly, raising children. As the morally superior and yet physically weaker sex, middle-class Victorian women were to be shielded from the corrupting influence of society at large.

This was demonstrated through the rights that women were afforded. Before the 1880s, when a woman married, her property passed to her husband's ownership and her individual legal identity ceased because she and her husband were considered to be one person under the law. In 1857, an Act of Parliament had made it easier for married couples to obtain a divorce; however, it ensured that doing so was much easier for men than women. For a man to obtain a divorce he needed only to prove that his wife had been unfaithful; for a woman to get a divorce she had to prove her husband's infidelity and cruelty. Historically, the custody of children also passed to men. That had gradually started to change from 1839 onwards, when women started to acquire rights of access and custody for children in certain cases; however, a husband essentially retained rights over his wife's body and the products of that ownership, which included children.

Many of those gradual gains in the legal status of women resulted from organised movements and campaigns. Arguably the biggest movement of the latter half of the nineteenth century was the campaign to grant women the right to vote. At the start of the century only a small percentage of wealthy men were entitled to vote; as the years went on, however, a series of reforms extended that right to more and more men. In 1866, a petition was presented to Parliament calling for women to have the same political rights as men, but the measure was defeated. Groups supporting women's suffrage emerged across the country and in 1897 a number of them joined together to form the National Union of Women's Suffrage Societies, led by Millicent Fawcett.

The campaign for women's suffrage can be broadly categorised into the 'suffragists', who campaigned through non-confrontational means, such as petitions and public meetings, and the 'suffragettes', who believed that radical methods were needed to achieve results. The Women's Social and Political Union, founded in 1903 by Emmeline Pankhurst, was a militant organisation that advocated for disturbances, such as window-breaking and arson, to command the attention of the press, politicians and public.[2] As a result of their actions, hundreds of women were imprisoned, and the many who went on hunger strike endured force-feeding by the prison authorities. In 1918 the vote was granted to women over the age of thirty who met certain property qualifications. Then in 1928 the franchise was extended to all women over the age of twenty-one, granting women the vote on the same terms as men.

One of the highest profile opponents of the suffragists' cause was Queen Victoria, and the significance of her reign to attitudes regarding women's rights must not be underestimated. She was perceived as the epitome of womanly virtue during her reign from 1837 to 1901. Despite her being the most powerful woman in the world, various comments attributed to Queen Victoria suggest that she thought women should stick to their domestic sphere. Victoria was devoted to her husband, Albert, and they had nine children together; however, when Albert died at the age of forty-two, she went into deep mourning and resisted public engagements. At that time, the Queen's withdrawal from public life attracted criticism and added weight to arguments that women were too volatile for public office.

The nineteenth century was even harder for women at the other end of the socio-economic spectrum. Working-class women had no choice but to work, often in domestic service or factories, to support their families, yet hours were long and wages were low. Housing conditions for the poor were crowded, although the only alternative for people who could not support themselves was to go into a workhouse. Gradually, however, working women organised into groups. In 1888, women and girls working at the Bryant and May match factory in London went on strike over unfair dismissal and their working conditions; eventually their demands were met and their strike led to the formation of the Union of Women Match Makers. Occasionally women from more privileged backgrounds had to work, usually as governesses, teachers or nurses, and some of those women were to form the vanguard for women's education.

In the first half of the century, the education of women in England was entirely piecemeal. A lucky girl may have been allowed to join her brother's lessons with his tutor, or attend the local church school, while others may have benefited from the instruction provided by governesses, but generally girls were schooled in only those 'accomplishments' needed for a blissful domestic life: music, drawing, dancing and needlework. Gradually, secondary schools were established to provide a more rounded education to girls, and by the end of the century universities and colleges were enabling women to study at a level never previously available to them.

GIRTON COLLEGE AND THE UNIVERSITY OF CAMBRIDGE

'A flowing river is no doubt more troublesome to manage than a tranquil pool; but pools, if let alone too long, are apt to become noxious, as well as useless.'[3]

Emily Davies, founder of Girton College,
The Higher Education of Women, *1866*

In 1869, Emily Davies co-founded the first English college to offer a degree-level education to women: Girton College.[4] Initially, the college's five female students lived in Hitchin, a town thirty miles south of Cambridge, taking classes from Cambridge lecturers who were supportive of their cause, but in 1873 the college and its fifteen students relocated to the outskirts of Cambridge. The building was designed by Alfred Waterhouse in a neo-Tudor style constructed out of red brick, and even the architecture seemed determined to challenge the status quo: in contrast to a lot of the older colleges, the rooms at Girton were arranged along corridors rather than around staircases.[5]

In the meantime, Newnham College had been set up as a home for women to live in while they attended lectures at Cambridge, yet the approaches and profiles of the two institutions differed markedly. Whereas Newnham allowed women to study at the level and pace that suited them, Girton aimed for its students to match the men from the outset. Emily Davies believed that the curriculum offered to women should reflect what was being offered to men, so the students at Girton took preliminary examinations before starting out on their chosen Tripos (honours degree).[6] They did so despite having no official recognition from the university, which took until 1881 to allow the women to sit its examinations formally (and until 1948 to award them degrees).

Almost from the outset, the University of Cambridge lagged behind other institutions in terms of women's education. In 1878, London University became the first to award women degrees, and affiliated colleges around the country offered women opportunities denied to them at the country's leading academic institutions. What accounts for Cambridge's reluctance to allow female students to study and graduate on equal terms to men? The university's tremendous history and the weight of tradition must certainly have played their parts.

The University of Cambridge was founded in 1209 and is made up of constituent colleges, the eldest of which is Peterhouse. Trinity College (where all the male characters in *Blue Stockings*, except Will, study or teach) was founded by Henry VIII in 1546, more than three hundred years before Girton was established. Cambridge therefore represents centuries of tradition and of educating the country's male leaders, scientists and poets. Until 1926 the highest governing body in the university was the Senate, which was comprised of all graduates.

From speaking to the King's College archivist, Jessica discovered that it was not until the 1880s that King's began to admit boys through merit. Before that it was entirely through privilege; if you went to Harrow or Eton, you did not have to sit the exam to get in, you just got given a place. In 1896, eighty per cent of the Fellows (the role that Mr Banks is offered at Trinity) would have been Etonians, and boys often brought their servants with them to college. She also discovered that King's College voted to allow lecturers to decide individually whether to allow women into their lectures or not, rather than imposing a blanket policy upon them.

When the question of admitting women to the university was first raised, it was perceived as a threat to tradition. Then, as now, Cambridge provided students with a rigorous, highly academic education and was one of the most respected higher-education establishments in the world. Admitting women, who would most likely not have had the same level of schooling as their male counterparts, posed a risk to that reputation. Moreover, the university was so ingrained in the livelihoods of the British Establishment that, for some, the fact that the women's colleges admitted students from a more diverse range of socio-economic backgrounds threatened the privilege they enjoyed – and the British class structure as a whole.

For the women who got to Girton, it nonetheless provided opportunities to study and socialise in ways that had been hitherto unimaginable. Along with those freedoms, there came responsibilities, and students found their days and nights regimented and regulated by college authorities, who were cautious not to allow any scandal to derail their mission.[7] It was also not unusual for a student's education to be interrupted by pressures from home. For example, Constance Jones, who later succeeded Elizabeth Welsh as Mistress of Girton, was in her mid-to-late twenties when she matriculated in 1875. Jones was the eldest of ten children and the education of her brothers was of higher priority; various interruptions to her studies meant it took her five years to achieve a first-class pass in her exams.[8]

Trips to Girton informed much of the early work on the play. When Jessica and designer Philip Engleheart visited Cambridge they subjected themselves to the 'Girton grind', walking uphill from the centre of town to Girton. When they finally reached the college, an unexpected entrance revealed how students might have snuck past the disciplinarians. 'There was a little short cut through some bushes, which I think is the way we got to it,' Philip says. 'Imagining that it was the exact way the lads would have got in, or the girls would have got out, was really exciting.'

Visiting Cambridge certainly helped actress Verity Kirk to understand what Girton would have meant to her character. 'Everyone always says that it is magical – and it is,' she says. 'Going into rooms where there are just books and books and books, you get the feeling of what that would have meant to somebody who loves to read.' To her, Cambridge 'felt like it had this legacy of learning that sucked you in and felt like the only place in the world.'

Jessica's Reflections on the Research Trip

In every production I've directed, I've tried, if possible, to do a relevant day trip. Not only can it offer great research opportunities towards understanding the world of the play, but it's a great opportunity to bring the company together and to help them all invest in the piece as a group. We visited a sheep farm for an adaptation of Hardy's *Far from the Madding Crowd*, and Austen's house for *Sense and Sensibility*, went to Bath for Sheridan's *The Rivals* and to an Iraqi centre for Judith Thompson's *Palace of the End*. So, of course, nothing would make more sense than for the cast and crew of *Blue Stockings* to spend the day in Cambridge.

We organised visits to the archive at both Girton and King's (an all-male college until the twentieth century), and also visited places featured in the play. But, I think, more than the specific fact-finding, to spend time in the city helps them to understand the scale of the fight. The college buildings are so grand and imposing, it's rather like standing amidst cathedrals. The air of formality, the scale of the architecture, the gown-wearing, the manicured lawns – it really hasn't changed much since the time the play is set. It was fascinating, and pretty incredible, to think the action of the play, to a large extent, really happened. To look at the window where they hung the mannequin. To work out which shop would have been the haberdashery where the confrontation takes place... There's a wooden-beamed, old-fronted shop right on the market square; I think it's there – I can almost see Holmes going in now to buy his gloves from Mrs Lindley. All in all, a very moving experience.

SCIENCE AND TECHNOLOGY

'The advantage of the emotions is that they lead us astray,
and the advantage of science is that it is not emotional.'

Oscar Wilde, The Picture of Dorian Gray, *1891*

The nineteenth century was a time of startling technological advancement following the Industrial Revolution of the previous century. The characters in the play would have directly benefited from developments, like the growth of the railway and steam travel; and would have been aware of major scientific discoveries, like the pasteurisation process. Yet recognising how recently life-changing technologies like the light bulb were invented also helps actors to appreciate how forward-thinking the characters are, and how the women's studies place them at the cutting edge of scientific endeavour.

The following is a timeline of the major scientific and technological advances in the years immediately preceding the time in which the play is set. It is based on a list of inventions that Jessica compiled during her preparation and shared with the actors:

1824   First public steam locomotive carries passengers.

1838   First photograph is taken using the daguerreotype process.

1839   Pedal bicycle invented by a Scottish blacksmith.

1840   Postage stamps are used in England for the first time.

1843   The first Christmas card is sent.

1844   The first Morse code message is sent.

1845   First inflatable rubber tyre designed.

1846   Discovery of the planet Neptune.

1850   The domestic Singer sewing machine is invented.

1852   First public flushing toilets open in London.

1853   Postboxes first used in Britain.

1859   Charles Darwin publishes *On the Origin of Species*.

1863   The first London Underground line opens for business.

1872   The penny-farthing bicycle is invented.

1873   The first typewriter with a QWERTY keyboard is manufactured.

1875   Cadbury makes its first chocolate Easter egg.

1876   Alexander Graham Bell is granted a patent for the telephone.

1878   Electric street lighting is first introduced in London.

1879   Albert Einstein is born.

    The light bulb is patented.

1883   Britain's first electric railway line is built in Brighton.

1885   First motor car built.

1886   Sigmund Freud sets up his clinical practice in Vienna.

1887   The Gramophone is invented.

1888   The Kodak camera and film is made available to consumers.

1894   Moving pictures ('the movies') first comes to Europe from America.

1895   First radio signal sent.

    The X-ray is discovered (as Edwards talks about in the play!).

Character Profiles

THE GIRTON WOMEN

TESS MOFFAT is a first-year student at Girton College in Cambridge. She is one of a small yet significant number of women who are studying at university level in the country at this time, and although the students at Girton take classes and examinations, they do not yet have the right to graduate. At Girton, Tess has a passion for astronomy and ambitions to travel across South America charting the stars. Her essay on Kepler is used as an exemplar by both Mr Banks and Mrs Welsh to demonstrate the academic capabilities of a woman's mind.

As a young girl, Tess was always hungry for knowledge. In Act Two, Scene Nine, she recalls climbing on to the roof of a local school so that she could eavesdrop on the lessons, which tells us that whatever minimal education she had access to was not enough for her. She admits she used to 'wreck Mother's nerves with worry' and if Tess was not initially allowed to attend school, perhaps that incident might have encouraged her parents to let her do so.[9]

We learn more about Tess's home life in Act One, Scene Eight, when she is visited by her childhood friend, Will Bennett, a student at King's College. Will has promised Tess's father that he will look out for her while she is at Cambridge, but tells her: 'Your father had no idea what he was sending you in to' (p. 43). Although Tess's parents are supportive of her studying at Cambridge, and have given her permission to do so, Will suggests that they would be uncomfortable with the recent events at Girton, as the college gears up to campaign for the women's right to graduate.

Although Girton might have appeared to be a place where women could go and study quietly, the graduation campaign will put it in the spotlight, perhaps nationally. Tess's parents would probably want to protect her reputation by making sure she is not associated with any political activity, particularly if the campaign has any association with suffrage. We might expect that Tess's parents would have sought to shelter her from such controversy when she was growing up.

Tess is unmarried and does not have children, although in Act Two, Scene Five, she tells Celia that she would like to be a wife and mother one day. In Act One, Scene One, Tess first tells Carolyn about Will. Later, Will declares his love for Tess, but she is unable to reciprocate as she has fallen for another student, Ralph. When Ralph meets another woman and decides to propose, it falls to Will to tell Tess. The play ends with Will promising to wait for Tess until she feels able to love him, but it is interesting to consider how and when Tess realises that Will could be the man for her.

Tess is the first student that the audience meets, and she is the central protagonist. The character evolved considerably during the writing of the play. In the early version of the script performed at RADA, the central protagonist was called Gertie Moffat; by the time the play was produced at Shakespeare's Globe, her name had been changed to Tess and the key events of the play were reshaped around her. In early drafts, the incidents of the play were more equally divided between the four female students; however, when redrafting for the Globe, Jessica ensured that the story was told more from Tess's perspective: 'I wanted the play to be more filmic, and films are almost always focused through one character's perspective. There's so much story to tell in *Blue Stockings*, I thought we would invest more fully if we were allowed to see the whole of one character's experience, rather than splitting our time. That's why I refashioned the play around Tess. And I changed her name because I thought "Gertie from Girton" just sounded silly!'

Jessica's Reflections on Writing for a Central Protagonist

This was the first play I wrote, and I learned, as I went from draft to draft, that it is easier to tell a complicated story through a single perspective. The audience really wants to invest in one person's story. I was also writing the film version at the same time and in a film you have to write for a single protagonist. It is the first rule of filmmaking that you ought to be able to write a logline along the lines of '*this* character who is in *this* situation is compromised by *this* person/event/fear, and has to combat that in order to achieve their goal'. So because I was rewriting it for film as Tess's story while we were preparing for the Globe production, it seemed natural to rework my playscript at the same time. The RADA version gave equal weight to the four women's stories, but I felt that there was too much going on and we never really got to know any one of the girls well enough. It was a shame not to write more for Celia, Carolyn and Maeve, but I wanted the clarity of emotional journey that you get from following one person in particular – and through Tess, we encounter the others.

CELIA WILLBOND is a diligent student in Tess's class at Girton; however, unlike the others, she is not new to the college. Celia is repeating her first-year studies after she was sent home suffering from nervous exhaustion – an experience that has taken its toll on Celia and affected her attitude to her studies and dealings with the other women.

In Act Two, Scene Five, Celia tells Tess: 'I worked through till dawn every night then went straight to prayers. I had to fight to come back. What would I have done if they'd said no?' (p. 86). She knows what it feels like to almost lose the chance of a university education, and she is not prepared to risk it again. Of all the women, Celia is the most mindful of propriety, Girton's rules and how the women are perceived by other people. She is not afraid to remind the others how they should behave – not that they take much notice!

Over the course of the play, Celia and Tess develop a special bond. Celia seeks Tess out in the orchard, and tries to encourage her back to her books when she is distracted or dispirited. Although she does not explicitly say so, it is likely that Celia has seen other girls find themselves torn between love and education before Tess; she therefore observes Tess's growing relationship with Ralph warily. Celia urges Tess not to make the same mistakes that she did, and risk throwing away this chance of an education. At first, Tess thinks that Celia does not understand her feelings for Ralph because Celia is not interested in romance. This hurts Celia who tells her: 'I mean, I've never had a Ralph. I want that too. Almost more than anything' (p. 86). The difference between them is that Celia has already realised what Tess ultimately has to learn: for now, getting an education is more important than falling in love.

Jessica's Reflections on Celia

I have a great deal of affection for Celia. She is the most conventional of the four friends, in terms of the Victorian stereotype of a woman. She is the softest of the four, and is the character directors tend to have the most questions about. Perhaps that's because she's quieter, and keeps her emotions a little more hidden. She is more reserved, because she needs to be. She had such a scarring experience in her first year, and is back at Girton to repeat it, so she has to get her head down and is worried about failing again. She's also seen a year of students, many of whom might have had difficulties, so she's much more attuned to the risks of studenthood. She is absolutely determined to succeed this year – she will not be allowed to retake again – and she does her best to persuade her friends that they must not take any risks if they don't want to suffer as she did. However, being a private sort of a person, she will avoid talking about the fact she is repeating if she possibly can.

I wanted Celia to seem starchy and quiet at first. She works hard, she's not a risk-taker and does not want the distraction of romance. She has seen how it can wreck an education. Every year there would have been girls at Girton who didn't come back for their second year, for a multitude of reasons. They may have become involved with a man, failed their studies, become ill, homesick, or found the pressure of study too much and been sent home. Celia is cautious because she has seen it all. There ought to be delight in the revelation that she wants romance like Tess does, but she knows this is not the time for that. Tess and Celia are similar in many ways; it's just that one of them has a year's more experience and has learned from it. I wonder whether there might be something of Celia's caution in Tess when she returns the following year.

CAROLYN ADDISON is one of a kind. Despite being in her first year at Girton, she has already travelled the world with her parents and thinks nothing of regaling the women with the wisdom she has learned overseas, such as the teachings of Greek philosophers, voting rights in Burundi, and Masai sayings. She is a firm believer in the empirical merits of science, and tells Lloyd that she plans to be a doctor once she finishes her degree.

As far as Carolyn is concerned, rules are there to be broken. She has snuck her wolfhound Achilles (named after the Greek hero, but perhaps an acknowledgment that Carolyn's desire for companionship is a hidden vulnerability) into the college, despite the fact that pets are not allowed, and acquires two more dogs on a whim in Act One, Scene Eleven. Carolyn is the first to encourage Tess out to meet Ralph in the orchard, and leaves Will and Tess unaccompanied in Act Two, Scene Two, despite promising Miss Bott otherwise.

Carolyn's upbringing has given her the air of a bohemian intellectual, and she displays the carefree extravagance of someone for whom money is no object. In Act One, Scene Three, she most explicitly draws attention to her wealth, which provokes a response from Maeve (pp. 25–6):

> CAROLYN. But it's not true, is it.
> MISS BLAKE. What isn't?
> CAROLYN. 'The simple life.' It's just sentimental puff that's said to make lower-class people feel better.
> TESS. You can't say that.
> CAROLYN. Oh come on. Who doesn't want material things? No one wants to live like a factory worker in some backwater out in the slums. Happiness is based on who you are and what you have.
> MAEVE (*suddenly standing*). You know nothing –

On a few occasions, outspoken Carolyn shows a slight lack of sensitivity to the feelings of the other women. As an only child who has spent her life trailing her parents around the globe, she is likely to have been schooled on her own and so has not spent much time with other women her age. That might also suggest a loneliness lurking behind Carolyn's exotic past; perhaps the desire for companionship is why she is so keen for Tess to join her family in Paris at Christmas.

MAEVE SULLIVAN is a first-year student at Girton. Whereas the other women confidently launch into eager discussion, Maeve has a quiet intelligence and often holds back before surprising them with her knowledge, insight and reasoning. She excels in Miss Blake's moral-science class and Mrs Welsh calls her an 'extraordinary student' (p. 59).

Maeve reveals little about herself or her home life. From comments made about her clothes, or the perspective she shares in class, there are occasional glimpses that Maeve does not come from the same social background as the other women; however, it is only when tragedy strikes that the full truth is revealed.

The pivotal moment for Maeve comes in Act One, Scene Eleven, when her brother Billy arrives at Girton, demanding that Maeve return home with him. It is evident that Maeve's family are very poor and Billy tells her: 'You're not one of them. Look at you' (p. 58). We learn that a benefactor, Lady Beaumont, pays Maeve's family an allowance so that she can study; if Maeve were not at Girton, she would instead be working and earning a wage to help support her family. We might assume that Lady Beaumont helped with Maeve's schooling before she joined Girton, and an earlier draft of the play revealed that Maeve used to work in service in Lady Beaumont's household. Billy then reveals that their mother has died and Maeve is needed at home to care for their younger siblings while Billy goes out to work. When Maeve refuses to return with him, Billy compares her to their father, who has abandoned the family. Mrs Welsh insists that Maeve must leave the college and care for her siblings, although Maeve puts up a fight and blames her poverty for how she is being treated (p. 61):

> MAEVE. It's cos of where I'm from, isn't it? Cos I'm not like them. Cos I needed help.
> MRS WELSH. You know perfectly well that's not true.
> MAEVE. You only want respectable girls from respectable families. Not slummers' drudge like me.

When Maeve finally leaves Girton at the end of Act One, the other women are deeply saddened. Even though she kept herself to herself, Maeve had impressed them all with her moral reasoning and made friends, for example by distracting Miss Bott while Tess and Ralph had their first rendezvous in the library. Maeve's departure from Girton is therefore a loss felt by all.

Jessica's Reflections on the Women's Relationships

For a relationship to be dramatically interesting, there must be a journey. People, friendships, relationships need to change and evolve. That's the drama. It is important that the women grow in their friendship as the narrative moves forwards, just as their learning grows through the lectures they attend.

Within the foursome, there are natural bonds that begin to form early on. Tess and Celia become friends from the off, as they see something in common with each other, whereas Carolyn's free-spirited nature makes her a little intimidating to the others. She's unpredictable, bolshie and could seem like a show-off. Maeve is very quiet, so none of the girls get the measure of her with any speed. She keeps herself to herself, but we should see that, as they spend time together, the others begin to learn more about her. They all start to enjoy each other's company, so that when Maeve leaves it has a devastating effect. Though these four girls would have had little in common and would probably not have been friends in the outside world, they all share the extraordinary experience of being students together and bond over their union against the opposition and their determination to win the right to graduate.

When Maeve leaves, Tess is really knocked by the loss of her friend, and shaken by Mrs Welsh's decision to let her go. Writing the film version of *Blue Stockings* has allowed me to explore this further. Part of the reason Tess begins to question everything at Girton is because Maeve's dismissal has made her question what the institution stands for. She feels that Maeve has been utterly compromised. There wasn't time to explore this fully in the play, but I think it's useful for an actor playing Tess to take this into account when looking at where her doubts come from and her growing lack of faith in Girton.

THE MEN

RALPH MAYHEW is a second-year student at Trinity College. He is a scientist and a romantic, who is sympathetic to the idea of women studying at Cambridge. After meeting Tess for the first time in the university library, the two embark on a romance that, although not entirely secret, is never made public.

At first, Ralph is not a conventional wooer. For their first meeting he invites Tess to a dark orchard, and when introducing himself to her for the first time he adopts the awkwardly formal title 'Esquire' (p. 50). In Act Two, Scene Three, we see them stargazing and Ralph admits that he has been distracted, but he does not say whether it was by the thought of Tess or by something else.

By Act Two, Scene Eight, we learn that Ralph plans to ask a woman called Eliza, who studies at Newnham College, to marry him. He has not told Tess. When Will challenges him, Ralph confesses that his father did not approve when he told him about Tess. Girton's radical stance and political reputation conflict with the expectations and plans that Ralph's father has for him. Ralph clearly comes from a traditional family and is destined for a high-profile future, which is not something Ralph necessarily wants. He tells Will: 'Listen, I'm a scientist, I wasn't cut out to be a politician. I didn't want this. I didn't choose it' (p. 99).

Nonetheless, Ralph has had to bow to his father's pressure and find a more respectable woman to marry. We see the effects of Ralph's decision on Tess, who is heartbroken, but when Ralph says to Will, 'If you see her, will you wish her well' (p. 99), it suggests that in letting Tess go, Ralph has lost something special too.

Jessica's Reflections on Ralph

Ralph could easily be misunderstood as a selfish cad, who toys with Tess's heart. I don't think this is the case at all. To me he is a romantic who falls wholeheartedly in love with Tess, but is too weak to stand up to his father, and therefore ends up taking the cowardly way out. To play him as a heartless cad who has just switched allegiances and fallen in love with someone else is to miss the point. The early scenes between him and Tess are entirely genuine. He finds her captivating and admires her bravery in standing up for what she believes in. It's just a shame that he isn't as brave as she is.

I imagine that, over the holidays, Ralph has returned home and told his parents he wants to marry Tess, only to be told that he must not. Tess is a student at Girton, which was seen as dangerous and political. His parents have their sights set on his marrying a good, respectable girl. He cannot risk his reputation, and to marry Tess would be to associate himself with a dangerous institution, activism and suffrage. He is about to embark on a respectable career and so reputation is everything.

When he tells Will to pass on his regards to Tess, it is a heartbreaking moment for him, so the actor should not play it as though it's an afterthought or isn't meant. When he says that Tess was special, what he means is that he loved her more than anybody, but he can't talk about it because it is too painful. That's why he covers his feelings with bravado in front of his friends. That conversation is Ralph putting on a front. He would have done almost anything to be with Tess, but the pressures of family and society were too much for him. He is not as strong as we would like him to be, but in writing I hope to reflect a sense of reality rather than a glossy view of the world. There would have been many men like Ralph who would have loved to marry the Girton girls, but felt that they couldn't. They weren't devils; they were just regular guys

> who had the weight of expectation on their shoulders. Not everyone can be a Will.

WILL BENNETT is a second-year student and Tess's childhood friend. It is the roof of his classroom that Tess climbed so that she could listen in to lessons. Although he is at King's College, Will takes Mr Banks's natural-science class with the Trinity students. Will's reputation at Cambridge is important to him as he is aware it may hold the key to his future employment prospects. Yet he quickly realises that his association with Tess and the Girton students lowers him in the estimation of men like Lloyd and Holmes, and he later reveals that he has been barred from the common room because he is friends with a bluestocking.

Clues in the text suggest Will does not come from quite as prosperous a background as some of his peers. He is not fully assured of a job upon graduating and tells Tess that it is important he passes with a first-class degree. At Christmas dinner, his family try to set him up with a Miss Pope, who is due to inherit her family's wealth and would therefore make a good match for Will.

Will, however, has fallen in love with his old friend Tess. In Act One, Scene Eight, he tells her that he has promised her father that he will watch out for her at Cambridge, and that he is worried about her risking her reputation. His loyalty is tested as he struggles with whether to warn Tess's father about the graduation campaign, but ultimately he does not do so. After he has spent Christmas with her family (while Tess is in Paris with Carolyn), he returns to confess his feelings for her. It is a blow when Tess tells him that she has fallen for Ralph, but when Will goes to speak to Ralph about his intentions towards Tess, he learns about Ralph's plans to propose to Eliza. Mindful of Tess's feelings, Will tries to put her off Ralph by saying he is not suitable for her, but when pushed he tells her about the other woman. Will continues to look out for Tess and the other women, and comes to Girton to warn them about the rioters.

Will and Tess have a spark and a familiarity that evolves over the course of the play. For Will and Tess to have a happy ending, the challenge is to show that he understands her better than anyone else. Tess may not always notice or appreciate it, but throughout the play Will is there for her, no matter what.

Jessica's Reflections on Will

Will represents home. He is the kindly boy-next-door – not the fantastic, romantic love interest who sweeps girls off their feet with love notes in libraries. He is, in many ways, our 'everyman'. He feels the pressure of society and, like the other men of his generation, is mistrustful of the notion of women studying. However, he is open-minded enough to shift his perspective as he sees his friend grow and change, and realises what this opportunity means to Tess. He switches camps over the course of the play, and is therefore central to our understanding of the debate.

In the RADA version, Will (then called Charlie) and Tess were brother and sister and it was Celia who he fell in love with. When I rewrote the play with Tess as the central protagonist, I shifted the relationship to make Will a family friend. Although that changed their relationship, Will still plays the brotherly role to Tess, which is why she never sees him as a potential suitor. They have a sibling-like relationship – they are easy with each other, joking and arguing, and for the most part, they are able to be very honest with each other. Then Will declares his feelings for Tess, and that's when things get complicated… and interesting.

LLOYD is a second-year student at Trinity College. From the outset, he and Holmes are the most vocal opponents of the women studying at Cambridge. From a modern-day perspective, it can be all too easy to see Lloyd as a misogynist and the play's 'bad guy'; however, it is important to understand that he has strongly held and arguably justifiable reasons to feel the way he does.

Lloyd comes from a privileged and illustrious background, and his father owns property in Cambridge. By his early twenties Lloyd is already able to talk of climbing the Matterhorn, one of the highest and deadliest summits in the Alps. He is competitive, and does not take kindly to being shown an essay by a woman that is better than his own. Like Ralph, Lloyd's family have high expectations for him, but that is accompanied by a pressure to work hard and achieve excellence. He is highly educated and has worked his whole life to get where he is, so he is not exaggerating when he says, 'We're not average men here. We are the future. The leaders. The establishment' (p. 88).

In Act Two, Scene Six, Lloyd articulates why women studying at Girton concerns him. He knows that the education the women have received is inferior to his own, so he questions their right to study in the same place, and with the same tutors, as him. Yet his remarks are also driven by fear. Lloyd genuinely considers the women to be a threat to the traditions that the country's reputation, wealth and politics have been founded on. Moreover, the women's right to graduate might be a threat to his own future prospects: Lloyd will rely on Cambridge's prestigious reputation when starting out in his career and thinks that if women are allowed the right to graduate, it will devalue his own achievement in the eyes of future employers.

Lloyd and the women are more similar than they might care to think. They are the most advanced scholars of their day, they are ambitious and hard-working and they want to shape the future; they just have different ideas about whose role in society that is. Nonetheless, Lloyd undeniably has a nasty streak and sometimes goes too far. He is particularly cruel to Carolyn when likening her to a prostitute, and is physically violent to Will and Mrs Welsh during the riot. Whether such behaviour is something that Lloyd is proud of, or struggles to reconcile with what it means to be a gentleman, is up to the actor to decide.

Jessica's Reflections on Lloyd

I think it's vital that none of the men are played as fiendish, and Lloyd is the greatest danger in that regard. He is the one who is cruellest to the girls and who undermines them viciously in public; however, that is because he is scared of change and fearful that he himself will be undermined by these women. His speech in the haberdashery comes entirely from a place of fear.

I imagine Lloyd has come from a long line of Oxbridge students and was educated at Eton. At this point in history, he would have had a free pass to take a place at Trinity without taking the entrance exams, because he was an Etonian. Having been brought up in such strict surroundings, with huge expectations on his shoulders, he then sees the privileged world he feels a part of compromised by petticoated, uneducated girls turning up and expecting to take their place in it. I think that Lloyd's father, and his father before him, were double-first scholars at Cambridge, and Lloyd is worried he will not make the grade. The arrival of these women compounds all his fears.

HOLMES is a second-year student at Trinity College. Around the other men he has a bravura that perhaps masks a more sensitive, artistic side. In Mr Banks's class, Holmes reveals he is a violinist in the chamber orchestra and a runner. As with the other men, his behaviour suggests a privileged upbringing and he buys the season's latest fashions from the haberdashery, which suggests that money is no object.

Unlike Lloyd, who never repents for his riotous behaviour, in Act Two, Scene Eleven, Holmes does apologise for how the Girton women have been treated. Although he can never agree with the idea of women graduating, he respects their courage and is ashamed at the violence of the riot.

Jessica's Reflections on Class Distinctions Between Men and Women at Cambridge

One of the problems for women asking to be accepted at Cambridge, quite apart from their gender, was their class. The girls were from a much more mixed social background than the men. The male students were from the upper echelons of society, while the women running the university courses would seek out clever girls from secondary schools all over the country. In any one class at Girton, you'd have likely found the daughter of a farmer and the daughter of an aristocrat. Cambridge had long been seen as an elite establishment, and it was proud of this reputation. The idea of letting in not only the women, but the poor, was horrifying.

EDWARDS is a second-year student at Trinity College. His attitude to the women being in Cambridge is more sympathetic than the others', yet whenever he tries to make the women feel welcome he is shut down by Lloyd or Holmes. Edwards often finds himself the butt of their pranks: Holmes dares him to speak to Celia, but he is frightened off by Miss Bott, then Holmes rigs the card game so that Edwards gets blind drunk. They also enjoy teasing Edwards about his girlfriend, Maudie.

Like Holmes, Edwards is ashamed when the riot gets out of hand and apologises to the women for the damage. He even goes so far as to say he does not mind the women being in Cambridge. When Edwards asks what the women plan to do now they can't graduate, he demonstrates the gulf between them. For the men, an education is about prestige, qualifications and recognition, without which it is worthless. For the women, an education is about being given the chance to learn, and the other things are just a bonus.

Jessica's Reflections on Edwards Singing 'The Last Rose of Summer'

I first heard that piece of music when working on Sebastian Barry's play *Andersen's English* at Out of Joint. When I heard it, I was struck by how hauntingly beautiful it was: simple in one sense, yet almost elegiac too. I wanted Edwards to break the expectations completely in that moment. He's the butt of the jokes, they're all teasing him, and then suddenly, when he sings, he draws on something unexpected: a sensitivity that hints at his ability to understand the girls' perspective later in the play. He's a man with hidden depths, so I wanted a little foreshadowing of that.

THE STAFF

ELIZABETH WELSH (1843–1921) was the Mistress of Girton College from 1885 to 1903. She is one of only two characters in the play (the other being Dr Maudsley) based on real historical figures, although it is important to remember that the characters portrayed in the play remain fictional constructs that have been written with a degree of artistic licence.

In historical fact, Elizabeth Welsh was born in County Down in Northern Ireland, although the play makes no explicit reference to this and it is not necessary for the role to be performed with a specific accent. In 1871, she joined Girton at a time when the college was still located in Hitchin, then left to build a teaching career before returning as a lecturer and working her way up to the role of principal.[10] When Mrs

Welsh reminds Tess of Girton's history and what is at stake in Act One, Scene Six, she therefore recalls her own personal history and long-term investment in the good of the college. In the play we do not learn much else about Mrs Welsh's past, although in Act One, Scene Eleven, Miss Blake suggests that Mrs Welsh is a widow whose husband died in war.

In the play, Mrs Welsh leads the campaign for Cambridge's female students to be given the right to graduate. First she must convince the university's Senate to grant a vote on the issue. Then, when they do, she does all she can to support the campaign in favour of graduation rights. This overriding objective sometimes forces Mrs Welsh to act in ways that she might not wish to in other circumstances. For example, at the end of Act One, she sends Maeve home so that no one can argue she is putting a woman's education above the well-being of children, which is not an easy decision for her to take.

Mrs Welsh is wary of the campaign for women's suffrage, which puts her at odds with Miss Blake. Although Mrs Welsh supports the idea that women should have equal voting rights to men, she believes that the suffragists' reputation for radicalism and violence could undermine their case for the right to graduate. Again, Mrs Welsh's position is firm and unwavering. After telling her not to talk about the suffragists to the students, Mrs Welsh forces Miss Blake to resign when she finds out that she has been disobeyed. Although a disciplinarian, resolute in the pursuit of her aims, Mrs Welsh shows a more caring side when the students need it, and is willing to bend the rules. When Tess fails her first-year examinations, Mrs Welsh makes an exception to allow her to return.

Act Two, Scene Eleven, is the only time we see Mrs Welsh lose control. She is humiliated by the men burning an effigy of a bluestocking, and confronts them despite Will's warnings. When she surveys the damage caused by the rioters, she sees the destruction of not only her place of work, but her home and life's purpose, which is why '*All her self-control bursts until she is like an animal*' (p. 113). It is only when she learns that the vote has gone against them that Mrs Welsh is truly lost for words.

DR HENRY MAUDSLEY (1835–1918) was a leading psychiatrist of his time. He was born in Yorkshire and studied at University College London before building his career working in a number of different asylums. Maudsley corresponded with the likes of Charles Darwin and was a prolific essayist on the theory of mental health. Nowadays, the Maudsley Hospital in South London, which he helped to establish by donating a significant sum of money, is a renowned training and research institution in the field of mental health.

Much of what Dr Maudsley says in the play is based on his historical writings, including 'Sex in Mind and in Education'.[11] Again, it is important to remember that rather than being an arch-villain, Maudsley is a man of his time who has firm reasons for thinking the way that he does. Maudsley's argument is that men and women are biologically different and that a woman's physiology and mind are adapted to her primary role in the world, which is having children. Mental taxation through academic study was thought to render women unable to fulfil that crucial function, which Maudsley argues will ultimately threaten the continuation of the human race. Like Lloyd, Maudsley therefore feels as though the very foundation upon which Britain and her Empire has been built is under threat by the education of women.

It is no wonder that Maudsley reacts the way he does when the women attend his guest lecture at Cambridge in Act One, Scene Four. He initially displays his opposition to their presence by calling on only the male students to contribute. When Tess counters Maudsley's argument with the example of the French neurologist Charcot, he expels her from the lecture. Again, it is interesting to consider whether Dr Maudsley's response is in fact justified. At first he does Tess the courtesy of meeting her on an intellectual level and asking what evidence she has for the claims. It is only when she says she has none and yet continues to disagree with him that he draws attention to her gender. Still Tess argues against him, and that leads Maudsley to send her out. Holmes's remark to Tess in the following scene that 'He had the floor and he was our guest' (p. 35) must make us consider that Maudsley may have been in the right, and Tess in the wrong.

Jessica's Reflections on Dr Maudsley

Maudsley makes some pretty unpalatable comments about women in the play, and many of them are taken verbatim from his writing. However, although they sound outrageous to our twenty-first-century ears, he was not making the statement out of cruelty. He was genuinely concerned about the future of the country, and passionately believed in preserving the institution of the family.

This seems far more reasonable when you consider that the family as an institution was already being shaken by social changes. Many feared the suffragettes and their notion of women as equal to men would destroy the institution of marriage. Society was already in a state of flux because of industrialisation. Everything was changing: people were moving from the countryside to towns, jobs were being replaced by machines, and women, seemingly, were deciding they wanted to work. Would that mean they wouldn't want to be mothers? That was a huge fear. Queen Victoria was the most significant exponent of the notion that women should remain at home and have babies. You can see why Maudsley wanted to protect that. It was not that he did not believe that women were capable; he just thought that, for the good of society, everybody needed to maintain their functional roles: men should do the work and women should bring up the babies.

MR THOMAS BANKS is a natural-science lecturer who teaches at both Trinity and Girton. Will has told Tess that Mr Banks is an 'eccentric' (p. 18), and in his classes he uses unconventional methods to inspire the students. In his own studies, Mr Banks achieved a double-first: an exceptional degree classification that requires excellence across the board. Yet he is modest and, when congratulated, attributes his students' successes to their own hard work rather than his teaching.

Mr Banks is a committed supporter of women's rights to education, even though it puts him at odds with other members of the university faculty. In Act Two, Scene One, Mr Banks is offered a fellowship at Trinity, a prestigious position that would grant him membership of the college's governing body. Yet he is reluctant to give up his external teaching commitments at Girton, as he feels that doing so would let the women down and that he too would lose out if he no longer taught them. The professors reveal that he was 'a controversial choice' for the post (p. 71) and are shocked when Mr Banks lets slip that he supports the women's campaign for graduation rights. On learning this, not only do the professors withdraw the job offer to Mr Banks, but they fire him from his current teaching post. Mr Banks has a family: a wife, called Rose, and daughters. Yet he confesses to Miss Blake that without his teaching salary from Trinity the family are struggling financially. At the end of the play, Mr Banks defends the college from the rioters and helps Mrs Welsh.

MISS ELEANOR BLAKE is a moral-science lecturer at Girton. She was previously a student at the college when it was located in Hitchin, having joined Girton at the age of eighteen and, as she says herself, never left. Miss Blake does not necessarily mean everything she says in class, but rather provokes reactions and thought from her students. The women excel in her classes as they learn to think for themselves, and like them Miss Blake is a free-thinker, which sometimes lands her in trouble.

Miss Blake supports the campaign for women's suffrage. She thinks the suffragists could be strong allies in Mrs Welsh's campaign for graduation rights; however, Mrs Welsh thinks that their methods are too radical. Defying Mrs Welsh's orders, Miss Blake tells Carolyn, Tess and Celia that a leading suffragist, Millicent Fawcett, is due to speak at a rally in Cambridge. When Mrs Welsh finds out, the two clash.

In her first class with the female students, Miss Blake challenges them to choose between love and knowledge, telling them that it was a choice that she herself had to make. Miss Blake is unmarried, and she knows she will never have a family of her own. Girton and its students are all Miss Blake has, which makes it all the more painful when she is forced to resign from the college. Even though Mr Banks urges her to apologise and be reconciled with Mrs Welsh, and Miss Blake does not know what she is going to do or where she is going to go, she stubbornly refuses to make peace.

PROFESSOR COLLINS is a senior lecturer at Trinity. He is one of three senior academics who offer Mr Banks the fellowship, but he admits that he needed convincing to do so. Collins is sceptical about the value of educating women, saying that: 'A fellow can't be seen to fritter away his time in the pursuit of ladies' "education"' (p. 71). In Act Two, Scene Ten, he is part of the examining board for the women's end-of-year examinations. When Tess struggles to answer a question, Collins gives her time and assistance, but to no avail. The stage direction that 'COLLINS *can't help smiling*' when Tess is allowed to stay at Girton suggests that, despite his earlier opposition, the women's academic prowess may have won him over to their cause (p. 108).

PROFESSOR ANDERSON, another Trinity lecturer, recommended Mr Banks for the fellowship and is said to have 'put a lot on the line' in doing so (p. 71). Unlike the other two professors, Anderson never expresses an opinion on the education of women, but his support for Mr Banks suggests that he does not entirely disapprove. Nevertheless, he is powerless to defend Mr Banks once it becomes clear that his loyalties lie with Girton.

PROFESSOR RADLEIGH is a senior academic at Trinity College. To explain why he is opposed to the idea of women studying, he talks of his own wife, who he says 'has a life she wouldn't give up' (p. 72). According to Radleigh, his wife gets fulfilment from socialising, running community fairs and volunteering with charities. The Girton students, on the other hand, are sacrificing all that in pursuit of their education, which will not even guarantee them the jobs as scientists that they aspire too. Radleigh ends by saying that he would not want such a life for his own daughters. Later, he joins Collins to conduct the women's examinations, but is a lot less generous to Tess when she is unable to answer.

MINNIE is Girton's housemaid, who is responsible for cleaning the rooms, lighting the fires and helping the women. She has a good relationship with the students and can be trusted to keep their secrets, whether that means helping Tess to sneak out at night to meet Ralph, or hiding Carolyn's dogs from Mrs Welsh. She is unlikely to have had the same level of educational opportunities as the female students have, and will come from a poorer social background than the likes of Carolyn.

MR PECK is Girton's gardener and all-round handyman. He is persuaded by Carolyn to take her into town to hear Millicent Fawcett speak. The students have Mr Peck wrapped around their little fingers and can persuade him to do anything they need, which leaves him perpetually terrified that his boss, Mrs Welsh, will find out.

MISS BOTT is the women's chaperone at Girton. Unmarried women had to be accompanied by another, usually older, woman when in public or meeting men, to guarantee respectable behaviour and maintain a sense of propriety. Miss Bott's job is to accompany the female students outside the college and supervise them when in the company of men, during which time she knits constantly. Other than the fact she is unmarried, we are not told much about her life before the events of the play; however, it is interesting to consider what her private feelings towards the female students might be and how they would be demonstrated in her relationships with them. On the surface, Miss Bott takes her job very seriously and will not leave Tess alone with Will when he comes to visit her; but, in Act One, Scene Eight, as Tess sneaks out to meet Ralph, we get a glimpse that Miss Bott might not be such a stickler for the rules as she makes out.

THE OTHERS

BILLY SULLIVAN is Maeve's brother and a labourer. He probably works in the shipping industry by taking ad-hoc casual work as it becomes available, whether sailing on ships as a member of crew or working in construction in the ship-building yards on the major rivers or coastal ports. As the oldest male, he is responsible for providing for the family, especially since their father abandoned the family. Unlike his sister, Billy is illiterate, and because he is unable to write he comes to Girton to inform Maeve of their mother's death and take her home with him. Having not seen Maeve for many months, and potentially never having stepped foot in somewhere like Girton before, he responds aggressively when she resists his demands. As the head of the family, Billy expects his sister to do as he says.

MRS LINDLEY runs a haberdashery in Cambridge. In Act Two, Scene Six, she sells Carolyn and Tess fabric to make a banner. She is aware of the upcoming vote on the right to graduate, and although her attitude to it is never explicitly stated, she might suspect that the women intend to use the fabric for their campaign. After Lloyd has delivered his angry tirade against the women, Mrs Lindley shows her solidarity with them by ordering him out of her shop. However, she is a leaseholder and Lloyd reminds her that the shop's premises are owned by his father. She cannot risk losing her livelihood, so she sells Lloyd the blue stockings that he has requested.

Practical Scene Synopsis

Play and improvisation are fundamental tenets of Jessica's approach in the rehearsal room. Exercises and games free actors from the pressures of being 'on-book' and enable them to explore style, character and performance skills in a physical and enjoyable way. Improvisation can also be used to explore the ideas and dynamics behind scenes and to further work on character or relationships.

After each scene synopsis there is a suggestion for a practical exercise, improvisation or rehearsal technique that can be used when working on *Blue Stockings*. Many of these were used in rehearsal for previous productions of the play. They can be used at different stages in the rehearsal process; however, the improvisations are likely to produce more helpful results if the actors are already familiar with the story and characters, because then they will be based on facts that are going to be shared with the audience. These ideas can be adapted to respond to the specific needs of a cast, or used as a jumping-off point for countless other ideas and exercises that actors might respond to (see the chapter Playing the Part for further suggestions on using improv in rehearsal). They should obviously be conducted in a safe physical environment after actors have warmed up physically and vocally to prevent injury or strain.

ACT ONE

Prologue

The first day of term at Cambridge University in the year 1896. Male scholars hurry from the train station as four women carrying suitcases emerge from the bustle of people and gaze at their destination: Girton College. Dr Maudsley and Mrs Welsh each make an address; Dr Maudsley lectures the men on his treatise, 'Sex in Mind and in Education', sharing his view that the female body and biology make women unsuitable for the world of academia, as Mrs Welsh welcomes the new female students to Girton.

In rehearsal:

Rather than converse with each other, Dr Maudsley and Mrs Welsh address the theatre audience, which stands in for two different audiences in the world of the play. When performing intercut speeches it is important that actors sustain each thought into the next line, even though they are not in direct dialogue. This fast-paced exercise, which we used at RADA once the actors were confident with their lines, helps to keep the text alive for the actors as they pass the energy between them. When the play was performed at RADA, Mrs Welsh had a slightly longer speech and her lines alternated with Maudsley's. Although in the final version of the play more weight is given to Maudsley's speech, it is important that the actor playing Mrs Welsh stays alert and present in her own sphere, which this exercise will help with.

A Game of Tennis

Ask the two actors to stand at opposite ends of the room, facing one another. Explain that they are going to speak the scene, while playing an imaginary game of tennis.

Get the first character who speaks to serve. The two actors should then mime hitting the ball back and forth to each other as they speak the scene. If the rally falls into a predictable or boring rhythm, remind them that great tennis players constantly move, feint and stay in the moment to return the ball.

Encourage them to match the vocal delivery of each line with their playing to try to beat their opponent. Get them to think about which of their own lines might be winning shots and which of their opponent's lines they have to work harder to return.

Jessica's Reflections on the Prologue

It is vital to get the tone of the first scene right, and that comes down to the actor playing Maudsley. He needs to deliver his lines seriously, and not for comic effect. If the actor plays Maudsley as a ridiculous chauvinist, the scene does not work. He is a credible academic whose action is to warn and educate his audience, not to entertain them.

On the first night at Shakespeare's Globe, we found that the audience was laughing. I was mortified because I didn't expect it. I thought people would be horrified by what he says. We worried that it would send the play off in the wrong direction and we might end up, accidentally, with a pantomime. Therefore, we asked the actor not to leave any gaps for laughter in that first speech, so that when he got to the end of a line, he carried on with the next line without breaking, even if people started laughing. This meant the audience realised straight away that they could not laugh and had to listen. There are elements of the play that are meant to be funny, but it's very important that it sets off on the right foot.

Scene One: The Laws of Motion

The female students – Tess, Maeve, Celia and Carolyn – meet for the first time on the grounds of Girton, all oddly dressed in bloomers. Tess is curious; Maeve does not say much; Celia reveals she is not new to the college; and Carolyn boldly gets them all on first-name terms. Their lecturer, Mr Banks, arrives and quizzes them before reappearing with a bicycle: a thoroughly modern invention that gives all the women quite a surprise. Mr Banks tells Tess to get on the bicycle, which she just about manages to do with help from the others. Tess has never ridden a bicycle before, but as she shakily starts to ride around, Mr Banks explains how she is demonstrating Isaac Newton's laws of motion. Tess picks up speed and cycles off before there is a crash in the distance, which does little to dent Mr Banks's enthusiasm.

In rehearsal:

It can be difficult to appreciate just how new and revolution-ary the bicycle was to women like Tess in the late-nineteenth century. Today's actors are likely to be perfectly familiar with riding a bicycle, so when starting work on this scene it might be helpful for them to be reminded of how people behave when confronted with something totally novel, alien and potentially quite dangerous. It might be interesting to brain-storm what the cast think the equivalent, most thrilling inventions of the modern day are.

This exercise encourages actors to see everyday objects in a new light by making the familiar unfamiliar. By participat-ing and observing each other, actors should get a sense of how people feel and behave when confronted with something new and unexpected, which they can use to inform their playing of the scene. Likewise, furthering the exercise to explore status in groups can be a starting point for rehearsing how the status dynamics develop between the women in this first encounter, and as they help Tess to ride the bicycle.

Something New

Ask the group to sit in a circle, facing inwards. Explain that you are going to show them an object that they might all think they are familiar with… but that they would be mistaken. Encourage them to open their minds and imagine that they have never seen the object or anything like it before. They have no idea what it does, what it is for, or even whether it is safe.

Explain that it is their task to discover what the object is for. To do that they must use all of their senses to find out what the object is like and how to use it. The aim of the game is to invent a use that is totally different to the object's actual function.

Place the object in the middle of the circle – try and pick something that has the flexibility to offer the actors a range of possibilities: a chair, a hat stand, a piece of clothing… a bicycle!

Ask one actor to begin by approaching the object. Encourage them to take their time to become familiar with it and discover its potential. Once they have settled on a use, and clearly demonstrated it to the group, repeat the exercise so that everyone has a go.

Encourage the actors to reflect on how they behaved with the unknown object. Were their movements and gestures tentative or bold? Did they hold it with a firm or hesitant grip? Did they examine it from different angles or with different parts of their body? Did they feel nervous or excited?

You can repeat the exercise so that pairs or small groups are tasked with discovering and inventing a different object collaboratively. Again, encourage those watching to reflect on how the group interact and help each other. Do some assume a higher status than others? How is that demonstrated during the task?

Scene Two: Sightseeing

Holmes, Lloyd, Edwards and Will Bennett, all students at Cambridge, watch something in the distance. Edwards swears that he has just seen a woman riding a bicycle, which Ralph, another student, confirms he has also seen. The men are amazed that such a sight should be seen in Cambridge.

In rehearsal:

This is the audience's first introduction to the male students at Cambridge, and the scene tells us a lot about their distinct personalities and attitudes to the women. Nonetheless, it is a short scene that follows seamlessly from the preceding one and, if music is being used to link scenes, it might make sense to continue it under the boys' exchange. During rehearsals at RADA, composer Laura Forrest-Hay used rhythm-based exercises to establish the energy of the boys' entrance and dialogue, which then fed in to her compositions, as well as helping the actors to strike off on the right energy.

Group Rhythm

Ask the actors to stand in a circle. One should start by impro-vising a short, simple rhythm, by tapping on their body, stamping, clapping or vocalising, which can be repeated by everyone. Once they have established the rhythm by repeating it a couple of times, the rest of the group should join in.

Then someone else (it might be easiest if it is the next person around the circle, but it could be anyone) should add a new phrase to the original rhythm. Again, they may need to repeat it a few times to give the others a chance to get the hang of it, but once the new rhythm has been established, everyone should join in.

Keep going until everyone has had a chance to add a phrase to the rhythm, which may now be quite lengthy.

Stop the actors and draw their attention to any interesting sounds or dynamics that were created. For example, hitting the chest will create a very different resonance to clapping. Did the rhythm speed up or slow down? Why so, and how did it feel for the actors?

Bring the actors' focus on to the given circumstances of the scene – where are they, what time of day is it, where are they are coming from or going to, who else is around? Encourage the actors to reflect on what phrases or energies in the rhythm best reflected the energy of their characters or the scene.

Repeat the exercise with the scene in mind. Encourage the actors to keep any phrase or rhythm that they felt worked well, and to try new things where appropriate. Once they have established a rhythmic sequence that captures the energy of the scene, encourage them to play with tempo and volume.

As rehearsals go on, and the actors get even more familiar with their group rhythm, it could be used as a warm-up before work on a scene, or taught to other actors and played under a rehearsal or improvisation.

Scene Three: The Happiness Equation

Miss Blake, a lecturer at Girton, welcomes Tess, Maeve, Celia and Carolyn to her classroom. She asks them whether knowledge is the path to happiness and urges Tess to convince them all that it is. As the women debate Socrates and Shakespeare, Miss Blake challenges them to say what they would choose – love or knowledge – and confesses that it was a choice that she had to make. Celia makes the case for a simple life, but when Carolyn responds that happiness is based on material wealth, Maeve, who has been silent, speaks out. Miss Blake cautions the women that the male students are more advanced in their studies, before telling them that Mrs Welsh is working to persuade the university's Senate to hold a vote on whether to grant female students the right to graduate. She sends them out with the task of learning the great philosophers and then, more importantly, thinking for themselves.

In rehearsal:

The challenge with Miss Blake's classroom scenes is to create a sense of great minds at work. The women are inspired and passionate about their lessons and there is an energy behind everything they say. Playing this warm-up exercise, once the actors are confident with their lines and cues, is a great way of establishing energy and promoting teamwork.

Keep It Up

Get a medium-sized ball and ask the actors to spread out around the room.

The actors must keep the ball in the air and not let it hit the floor. They can use any part of their body to hit the ball into the air, but no one is allowed to hit it again until every other player has touched it at least once.

Get the group to count each touch of the ball as the game progresses. If the ball hits the ground, the counting should start again from zero. The aim is always to beat the previous highest score.

Once the actors are confident with their lines, get them to run the scene while playing the game. Aim to get to the end of the scene without the ball hitting the ground – if it does, go back to the beginning.

Scene Four: The Wandering Womb

The male students talk about a new scientific discovery as they arrive in a busy public lecture hall, followed by the female students who are accompanied by their chaperone, Miss Bott. Lloyd and Holmes dare Edwards to speak to the women, but when he approaches them Miss Bott advances, wielding her knitting needles. Mr Banks's arrival spares the tongue-tied Edwards any further humiliation. Mr Banks announces the prestigious speaker, Dr Maudsley, who is in Cambridge to lecture on the condition of hysteria. As he begins his address, Dr Maudsley invites the male students to impress him with their knowledge of the symptoms of hysteria. Lloyd alludes to Dr Maudsley's theory that hysteria is seen in women with weak morality. As the men share a joke, Tess intervenes and refers to an alternative theorist, who states that hysteria is caused by biology and not poor moral judgement. Dr Maudsley takes exception to Tess speaking without having been invited, and disagrees with her. As both their tempers flair, Dr Maudsley uses Tess as an example of a hysterical woman and orders her out of the lecture hall. She leaves the other women behind as Dr Maudsley makes his final point that mental exertion leaves women incapacitated as mothers.

In rehearsal:

It is all too easy for this scene to fall into a predictable rhythm and pattern, whereby the lecture starts off quite serious and dull, and then Dr Maudsley and Tess's voices rise in pitch and speed as they argue. However, the truth of the scene is much more exciting than that: Dr Maudsley is one of the most exciting minds in society, the students have been waiting a long time to hear him speak, and what happens takes everyone by surprise.

Singing the Scene

An exercise that Jessica uses to keep scenes fresh and surprising involves the actors singing a scene.

This works best once the cast know the lines, which they should sing in an agreed musical style – jazz works well for this scene because the improvised rhythms capture the sense of characters thinking on their feet.

The cast should be encouraged to listen to, and surprise, one another with their intonation, rhythm and volume, and when they pick up on cues.

Reassure them that it is not about producing something musically harmonious, but about revealing new and different ways of delivering lines to get interesting effects.

Scene Five: Out Without Hats

Carolyn, Celia and Maeve rush outside to join Tess after she has fled Dr Maudsley's lecture. Tess spots her friend from home, Will Bennett, walking past and joins him. Lloyd, Holmes and Edwards tell Will what happened in the lecture and berate Tess for having argued with Dr Maudsley. Miss Bott finally catches up with the women and ushers them away from the men who, having learned that Will is friends with the Girtonites, stop him from walking with them.

In rehearsal:

In this awkward encounter between two old friends, both end up humiliated. Tess has just been publicly embarrassed by Dr Maudsley, which is reinforced by Lloyd and Holmes's jibes, and Will finds himself ostracised by his friends because of his acquaintance with Tess. This improvisation will help the actors playing Tess and Will to explore their relationship in happier circumstances. It may make them think about the hopes they both had for their time in Cambridge together, and how this encounter fails to live up to those expectations.

Improvisation Outline

Time: Late summer.

Place: The parlour of Tess's home.

Characters: Tess and Will, plus another actor to play Tess's father.

Given circumstances: It is the last time Tess and Will will see each other before leaving for Cambridge. Tess wants to know what the lecturers, classes and libraries are going to be like, and Will knows they will have one lecturer in common: Mr Banks. During the scene, Tess's father comes in to speak to Will about his concerns over Tess going to Cambridge.

Scene Six: Fragments of the World

Tess is in Mrs Welsh's office following Dr Maudsley's lecture. Mrs Welsh tells her about the struggles they went through to build Girton into the place it now is. She explains that if the Senate agrees to a vote, and if that vote goes in favour of female graduation, Tess will be one of the first women ever to do so. Tess says that she is at Cambridge to understand the world so that she can explore and study it. Mrs Welsh explains that, as women, knowledge is the only thing they can ever truly own, and advises Tess to be sensible in her approach to those who may disapprove of her being there.

In rehearsal:

This scene can be deceptive. Unlike the incident in the lecture hall, Tess and Mrs Welsh largely see eye-to-eye and their tempers are not particularly raised. Yet, the stakes of what might happen for both women if the incident in Dr Maudsley's lecture is repeated are very high: if they are denied the vote that Mrs Welsh has been campaigning for, Tess and other women like her will be even further from the right to graduate. Mrs Welsh says that they are on 'the brink of acceptance' (p. 37), but that is a very precarious and uncertain place to be. Indeed, she even suggests that the college itself might be at risk if scandals continue.

We have all heard directors say, 'Raise the stakes!' But what does that actually mean to an actor, and how can they raise stakes in practice without crassly resorting to increasing volume and speed? Actors might find that objectives help to precisely communicate the high stakes of this scene. For example, there is a difference between Mrs Welsh's objective in this scene being *to make Tess understand the error of her ways* and her objective being *to ensure Tess never behaves that way again*. Likewise, for Tess there is a difference between her objective being *to explain what happened to Mrs Welsh* and her objective being *to keep her place at Girton*. In both cases, an actor playing the latter objective clearly and strongly will communicate much higher stakes to the audience.

Scene Seven: The Dictionary

Everyone is working in the library: the male and female students are at their books, Miss Bott is knitting and the Librarian is making sure everyone keeps quiet. Ralph and Tess catch each other's eye and he surreptitiously slips a note into the book that she is reading. When the note falls out of the book, Maeve deliberately creates a disturbance to distract Miss Bott as Tess retrieves it. Tess goes behind a shelf of books, pretending to look for a dictionary, where Ralph is waiting for her. They talk secretly, watched by everyone except Miss Bott and Celia, who is oblivious to it all and absorbed in her reading. Tess and Ralph emerge from behind the bookshelf, and he leaves the library as Tess rejoins Carolyn and Maeve at the table. They are desperate to get the gossip, but Miss Bott will not let them leave until Celia is finished too... which might be some time.

In rehearsal:

Rehearsal tasks can be used for deepening an actor's under-standing of their character's life beyond the action of the play. Ask the actors to write college reports for their charac-ters. Each character is different: some have great strengths and natural talents; some are excellent at one subject and dire at another; and others are hanging on by their toenails. The actors might imagine, for example, that Ralph has a gift for natural science but little literary prowess; Lloyd is under huge pressure to do well from his overachieving father, but has to work hard to get the grades; and Holmes is more of a sportsman and plays the violin brilliantly, so he is clever but unfocused.

They might like to include a social report as well. What is their character doing socially, for the life of the college, or in sports? How do they seem in terms of pastoral care? The actors playing the college staff could write such reports for the students in their care. For example, Miss Blake could write a paragraph on how each of the women is doing in her class, and Miss Bott might write a paragraph about their welfare.

The exercise will also get actors thinking about how clever the characters are (encouraging the quickness of wit that other scenes rely on), and what things they would typically be studying and encountering at Cambridge.

Scene Eight: The Great Escape

Tess is working in her room when Minnie, the maid, knocks on the door to tell her that a man is waiting to see her. Think-ing it might be Ralph, Tess douses herself in perfume and is a little disappointed to find that it is only Will. Miss Bott hangs around to supervise Will and Tess as they try to talk. Will tries to apologise for what happened earlier in the street and cautions her about what people say about Girton's stu-dents. He reveals that he has promised Tess's father that he will watch out for her, and that he plans to warn him about the controversy surrounding the vote on the women's right to graduate. After urging him not to write to her father, Tess makes Will leave.

Tess resolves to go and meet Ralph, and Carolyn comes in to find her with her coat on ready to go out. Carolyn senses that Tess is upset after seeing Will, and invites her to spend Christmas with her family in Paris. Maeve and Celia come to Tess's room; Celia warns her not to risk meeting Ralph, but Carolyn urges her on. The women are plotting how to get Tess safely out of the window when Minnie arrives and offers to help her escape through the kitchen, so they sneak past Miss Bott, who is asleep (or perhaps just pretending to be!) in the hallway.

In rehearsal:

This scene reveals the different attitudes and backgrounds of the female characters. Ask the actors to write a rough point-by-point history of their character, thinking about where they come from, who their family members are and what their key life experiences have been. The actors should look for facts or lines in the play that hint at the sort of life the character has beyond the action of the play itself. We know, for example, that Tess used to climb onto a roof to listen to Will's classes. What might that say about her and the place she was brought up?

Here is an example for Carolyn. Remember: it is a fictional history, and only one possible version of her backstory.

> Born 1878 in India. Lived there until she was three whilst her father, a well-to-do English gent with a lust for adventure, worked for *The Times of India*.
>
> Her parents met in Paris. Her mother is a well-known French opera singer.
>
> Carolyn moved with her mother back to Paris at the age of three, while her father went between the two countries. Sometimes Carolyn was passed from aunt to aunt and lived

with relatives when her parents were too busy with their respective jobs.

Her childhood was full of wonder. She used to sit in her mother's dressing room; dressers at the theatre acted as maternal influences. One of the grande dames of the opera world would read to her backstage, telling her tales of great heroines. This piqued Carolyn's interest in both literature and the wider world.

She was privately tutored from the age of seven. She moved with her family to Zurich at the age of eight. They always went back to Paris for the summer, where Carolyn was allowed to wander as she pleased and always given plenty of pocket money to make her own way in the city.

Her parents were argumentative. It was not a quiet home and they used to row regularly, but equally they would have huge amounts of fun. They were extravagant people, always holding parties, literary salons, inviting the who's who of contemporary society. They would drink expensive wine and argue about intellectual topics. They were a feisty group.

The family moved back to London when her father temporarily took over *The Times*. London was a lonely time for Carolyn. She had two-month trip to Sweden where she began drinking, smoking and finding her feet as a young woman. She lived in Rome for a time. She went to Vienna at fourteen and met Freud. No wonder she thinks she knows a lot!

Her life has been constantly on the road. Her family have always had money, and she has had what she wants, been to the best parties, travelled the globe and met hugely influential people – but is that enough? If she is really honest, she would often have thrown it all in, if she had the choice, for the stability of a simple family life and parents who had time for her. She is an only child.

Scene Nine: The Garden of Eden

Ralph waits for Tess in the orchard at Girton College; it is dark and she moves cautiously between the trees, unaware that he is there. Ralph makes Tess jump as he greets her, and he apologises for inviting her somewhere so spooky. They learn each other's names for the first time and Ralph reads Tess an Italian sonnet by the late-thirteenth-century poet Dante da Maiano.[12] They talk about the work of the astronomer Kepler, before Ralph says that it is good the women are studying at Cambridge. Before leaving, Ralph slips the poem under Tess's hat for safe keeping and, alone, she revels in the delight of young love.

In rehearsal:

In this scene, Ralph and Tess are both in a novel situation that they find surprising and not entirely comfortable, and they discover things about each other. The rehearsal technique of 'feeding-in' (or 'reading-in') can help actors to discover that freshness and spontaneity by enabling them to play each thought or 'beat' without being tied to the script. It can be used relatively early on in the rehearsal process, when actors are familiar with the shape of the scene and their character's objectives but do not yet know their lines off by heart. The technique involves actors running the scene without their scripts in their hands, while other actors stand on the sidelines and feed them their lines thought by thought.[13] The actors in the scene are therefore able to focus on playing, listening and reacting to each beat rather than getting distracted by the process of reading their lines. The practice is outlined in detail in the director Mike Alfreds's book *Different Every Night*, where it is placed in the important context of his rehearsal work on objectives and beats.

Jessica's Reflections on 'The Garden of Eden'

Ralph is an awkward wooer. He hasn't much experience, and the scene plays best when we see two people struggling with the awkwardness of a rendezvous. However, Ralph's genuine concern for Tess getting cold and his thoughtful gestures speak of his real feelings, and it's clear they both find each other captivating.

I like the idea that both Tess and Ralph have read romance novels but neither has experienced it in their own lives, so they're testing it out together. Ralph thinks it's romantic to bring an Italian poem, but hasn't thought it through... and gets caught out when she asks him to translate it. I thought that as someone who doesn't know much about poetry, Ralph would probably plump for a famous Italian writer when looking for something romantic. I didn't want him to be too original in his choice, because he doesn't even understand it!

Although Ralph can be played as a smooth operator, it is far more interesting to play him as someone who is not used to taking girls out. When he says that he should have taken Tess to a clarinet concert, and that he is an idiot for bringing her to a spooky orchard, he is being honest. Likewise, when he says that he is impressed by Tess choosing to study, he means it. There is nothing false in what he says to her at any point. If the actor plays it in a way that suggests that he's had a game plan from the beginning, it is boring. The scene needs to be played in the belief that Ralph really likes her, because then it is much more affecting when he lets her go.

Scene Ten: The Merits of Moral Science

Miss Blake is fired up after the women tell her they have been turned away from yet another lecture. She tests them: what is the point of her teaching them moral science, when advances in science and technology require their intellects? A lively debate ensues over the relative merits of science and art. Carolyn argues that art makes life worth living, while Celia and Tess argue that science keeps us alive. Maeve silences them all with another sudden outburst saying that great scientists think like artists and great artists approach their work like a science. That is exactly the kind of independent thought that Miss Blake has been looking for, and she praises the women for learning to think for themselves.

In rehearsal:

Like Scene Three ('The Happiness Equation'), this scene captures the quick wit and passion of the women's discussions; however, by this point in the play they are more confident in their own views and their relationships, both with each other and with Miss Blake. This is the scene where they really take off intellectually and start to think for themselves, and Miss Blake might notice that and enjoy a private moment of satisfaction. One means of exploring that sense with the actors might be to give them a debate topic like 'What is Happiness?', and allow them several days to research it before staging the debate in character. This will encourage them to think deeply about the characters' attitudes; however, by freeing them from the text it will also help them to experience the speed and stakes of a real debate.

Jessica's Reflections on 'The Merits of Moral Science'

My tip for directors is that the scenes featuring Miss Blake should be played energetically, like a tennis match, where the ball is always kept up in the air. The actors should pick up on one another's cues and be biting at the end of each sentence for a gap to say something, because that way we get a feeling of their spark. These are feistily intelligent women who have been chosen from far and wide to be part of this college because they have quick minds. If it is played like that, as though they are not only capable of keeping up, but also delight in the vigour of the process, it can be really exciting; however, if it is played like a boring classroom scene... it will be just that.

Scene Eleven: An Arrival

Carolyn asks Minnie to hide two Afghan hounds that she has bought, despite the college's rule that pets are not allowed. Minnie jokes that she has sold Carolyn's other dog, Achilles, but before Carolyn can respond, the arrival of Maeve's brother Billy interrupts them. Minnie calls Mrs Welsh, who tries to calm Billy down when he angrily demands to see Maeve. Billy tells Maeve that she has to leave Girton and come home with him, which she refuses to do. Mrs Welsh reminds Billy that their family are paid an allowance by a benefactor so that Maeve can study, but Billy reveals that their mother has died and that Maeve is now needed to look after their younger siblings. Shocked by this news, Maeve still refuses to go with Billy and he leaves angrily.

Once Billy has gone, Mrs Welsh tells Maeve that she will have to leave Girton and look after her siblings because their well-being is more important than her studies. Maeve tries to argue as Carolyn, Tess, Celia and Miss Blake look on, but Mrs Welsh will not budge. After the students have left, Miss Blake tries to persuade Mrs Welsh to change her mind, but the discussion turns to the issue of women's rights and the all-important vote. Miss Blake supports the suffragists, who Mrs Welsh thinks could undermine the case for the women's right to graduate, so she tells Miss Blake to have no further association with their cause.

In rehearsal:

Although this is the only time we see Billy and Maeve together, a strong grounding in their relationship will enable the actors to explore the full depth of emotion in this scene. The following improvisation has the potential to explore Billy's feelings about Maeve going to Cambridge, as well as how Maeve feels about having Mrs Welsh in her home.

Improvisation Outline

Time: Late afternoon.

Place: The Sullivans' home, which is small, shabby and sparsely furnished.

Characters: Mrs Welsh, Maeve, Billy, and another actor to play their mother.

Given circumstances: Maeve has spent the whole day cleaning the house for Mrs Welsh's visit, who has come to obtain Maeve's mother's permission for her to study at Girton. During the scene, Billy arrives home from a long day at work. He does not yet know who Mrs Welsh is, or that Maeve has been offered a place to study at Cambridge.

Scene Twelve: Science of the Heart

The male students are in Mr Banks's natural-science class. He hands back their essays and observes that, although academically astute, the essays lack the passion required for excellence. Mr Banks encourages the men to reveal what gets their own blood pumping. For Holmes it is running and playing in the orchestra; Lloyd remembers climbing a mountain in the Alps; Edwards and Ralph reflect on the sensation of being in love.

Elsewhere, Tess writes at her desk. As she finishes, Mr Banks gives the men a copy of another essay. They marvel at the passion shown by its writer and ask if the student who wrote it is also at Trinity, to which Mr Banks replies that it was written by a student from Girton. The men are dumbstruck that a woman should be capable of writing such an essay.

In rehearsal:

The male students, like the women in Miss Blake's class, ooze confidence and get a buzz from debating, and the language they use is deliberately chosen to have an effect: it may be to persuade someone of a point of view, to elicit an answer, to provoke a disagreement or to impress. Jessica uses the following exercise when directing Restoration and Georgian comedies, such as Richard Brinsley Sheridan's *The School for Scandal*. Those plays may date from before the nineteenth century, but the similarities with *Blue Stockings* are clear. In *The School for Scandal* the characters use language and wordplay to ridicule others. In the society of gossip-mongers, the ability to deliver a cutting remark or witty put-down is social currency; like the Cambridge scholars, those characters are judged on how confidently and cleverly they express themselves. The exercise encourages actors to speak with confidence and clarity, and they should be able to recognise the difference between delivering a line with consistent energy, and only partly committing or allowing the line to trail off.

Holding the Line

Ask the actors to stand in a large circle, facing inwards, and to choose a line that they speak in the play that is neither too short nor too long.

The first person speaks their line with an energy that reaches right across the circle. As they speak, they should also walk across the middle of the circle to take the place of someone standing opposite.

Whoever's place they have taken will then do the same thing, walking across the circle while saying their line before taking the place of someone else… and so on.

If the first few attempts are a bit lacklustre, stop the exercise and draw the actor's attention to where in the journey across the circle the energy dropped. The actors should be reminded to keep the energy up for the entire length of the line and the last word should be as punchy as the first, rather than the line tailing off at the end. Likewise, they should really connect to the person they are walking towards by imagining that they are trying to push the other person backwards using only the strength of their words.

Keep the exercise going until energy is consistently maintained by everyone.

Scene Thirteen: An Education

Mrs Welsh addresses the members of the university's all-male governing body, the Senate. She holds a copy of Tess's essay in her hand and reads from it aloud. The essay claims to solve an ancient mystery: it fuses a study of Johannes Kepler's physics and astronomy with biblical texts to explain the existence of the Star of Bethlehem. Elsewhere, Celia, Carolyn and Tess gather to bid farewell to Maeve as she leaves the college. Mrs Welsh concludes by asking the Senate to grant a vote on the women's right to graduate, as Maeve walks out the door.

In rehearsal:

Just one night has passed between Maeve learning that she has to leave Girton and her departure, yet in that time all the women will go through a significant emotional journey. This improvisation explores how the women spent that time, and might reveal how their relationships change following the news of Maeve's departure.

Improvisation Outline

Time: The evening before Maeve is to leave Girton.

Place: Maeve's room at Girton.

Characters: Maeve, Minnie, Carolyn, Celia, Tess, Miss Blake.

Given circumstances: Maeve is packing up her belongings with Minnie's help. Miss Blake wants to speak to Maeve before she leaves. During the scene, Carolyn, Celia and Tess arrive with presents for Maeve.

ACT TWO
Scene One: An Offer

Mr Banks is meeting three senior colleagues, Radleigh, Anderson and Collins, at Trinity. They offer him a prestigious permanent position as a fellow of the college, on the condition that he gives up his teaching at Girton. Mr Banks is reluctant to go back on his commitment to teach the women, which frustrates the senior fellows. When Mr Banks reveals that he is in favour of the women's right to graduate, Radleigh argues that having an education will harm their futures as wives and mothers. The professors leave, making it clear that Mr Banks is no longer in their favour.

In rehearsal:

It is possible for the roles of Radleigh, Anderson and Collins to be doubled with others, yet in doing so it is important that the roles are clearly differentiated. At RADA, costume and make-up were used to age the actors and make these characters visually distinct from the younger students, but performance technique also played an important part. The older characters were a lot slower in their movements and sat stiller in their chairs than their younger counterparts; likewise, their vocal delivery was more measured and deliberate. If doubling up, it might be interesting to run this scene a few times and experiment with playing the roles at a range of different ages. How does the meaning of the scene change when Radleigh, Anderson and Collins are just a few years older than Mr Banks, compared to their being played as men in their seventies? Likewise, are Radleigh, Anderson and Collins necessarily all the same age, or might portraying them as different ages highlight the different attitudes between the generations?

Scene Two: The Telescope

Tess, Carolyn and Celia dance the cancan with their petticoats scandalously on show.[14] Miss Blake and Miss Bott escort Will, who has a present for Tess, into the room and the shock of his appearance makes Celia trip and the cancan come crashing down. Miss Blake informs the women that the Senate have granted Mrs Welsh's request for a vote on the right to graduate, but that only current graduates (who are all men) will be allowed to vote. Before leaving, she tells them that the suffragist Millicent Fawcett is due to speak in Cambridge, but encourages them to keep it quiet from Mrs Welsh, who does not approve. Tess and Carolyn give Miss Bott snails that they bought in Paris and she helps Celia, who has injured her ankle, out of the room. Carolyn is left behind to supervise Tess and Will, but as soon as the coast is clear she leaves them alone. Will gives Tess her Christmas present – a telescope – and confesses that he has fallen in love with her. Surprised, Tess tells Will that she has met someone else. Will is curious, but does not want to know who she has fallen for. He makes his excuses and is about to leave when Mrs Welsh comes in. Finding them alone, she tells Tess off for dancing the lewd cancan and instructs Will to leave.

In rehearsal:

A lot happens during the Christmas holidays, including Tess and Carolyn's adventures in Paris, and Will working up the courage to tell Tess how he feels. Improvising things that have happened during that time can give actors an understanding of how those experiences might have influenced them. This improvisation explores Tess's family Christmas in her absence.

Improvisation Outline

Time: Christmas morning.

Place: Tess's family home.

Characters: Will, plus other actors to play Tess's parents, Will's parents and Miss Pope.

Given circumstances: Will and his family spend every Christmas with Tess's family, but this is the first time she has not been there on Christmas Day. They are all interested to hear about how Tess is getting on, and Will has to decide whether to tell Tess's parents about the campaigning – and about Ralph.

Scene Three: Time Travellers

It is later the same evening and Tess and Ralph are on a hill-top in Cambridge, gazing at the stars.[15] Ralph reveals that he has had something on his mind, and Tess assumes he means her, but might it be something else?

In rehearsal:

At Shakespeare's Globe, as in Shakespeare's time, scenic effects are often used sparingly and changes in time or location are instead communicated through language. That is evident in this scene, which Jessica wrote for the Globe production. From just the first two lines we know that Ralph and Tess are high up, as they can see all of Cambridge, and then we learn that they are outdoors and it is night-time.

Improvisation can be helpful to flesh out a short scene such as this one, which explores what might have happened in the time that has passed since Tess and Ralph last saw each other.

Improvisation Outline

Time: The evening that Ralph has arrived home from Cambridge for the Christmas holidays.

Place: The drawing room at Ralph's family home.

Characters: Ralph, plus other actors to play his father and mother.

Given circumstances: After every term, when Ralph arrives home, his parents question him about his studies, but this time Ralph is eager to tell them about Tess and get their blessing before he asks her to marry him. However, Ralph's father studied at Trinity and has just found out that the Mistress of Girton is leading a campaign to grant women the right to graduate.

Scene Four: Bread and Circuses

Carolyn tries to sneak out of the college disguised as a man to go and hear Millicent Fawcett speak. Before she and Mr Peck make it out the door, they are spotted by Mrs Welsh, who is angry to hear where Carolyn is going. When Mrs Welsh finds out that Miss Blake has told the women about the rally, she forces Miss Blake to choose between Girton and the suffrage cause.

In rehearsal:

The staff at Girton are rarely seen together, and Mrs Welsh and Mr Banks do not have any scenes together until the riot, when he comforts and supports her. When characters do not have many scenes together it can be helpful to explore relationships through improvisation such as this one.

Improvisation Outline

Time: Shortly before the start of term, during the Christmas holidays.

Place: The staffroom at Girton.

Characters: Mrs Welsh, Miss Blake, Mr Banks, Minnie.

Given circumstances: The staff of Girton are having a staff meeting to discuss lessons, Maeve's departure and the other students' progress before the new term starts. Miss Blake has just found out that Millicent Fawcett is soon to speak in Cambridge. During the scene, Minnie arrives with a letter for Miss Welsh, informing her of the Senate's decision to grant the vote.

Scene Five: Outcasts

Tess is meant to be revising the naturalist Georges Cuvier ahead of her exams, but instead Celia finds her sitting in the orchard trying to write a love poem. Carolyn has already told Celia that Tess has failed her botany exam, so Celia accuses Tess of letting Ralph distract her from her studies. Tess feels that what she has with Ralph might be more important than her education; after all, no other man will want to marry her now that she is a bluestocking. Tess hurts Celia by suggesting that she does not understand what it means to be in love. Celia replies that she longs for romance, but knows what it is like to lose the chance of an education because she is repeating her first year after working herself so hard she was sent home suffering from nervous exhaustion.

In rehearsal:

Celia says that she 'had to fight to come back' to Girton (p. 86), which would have been a pivotal moment in her backstory. Ideally, the actor will already have conducted some research on the causes and symptoms of nervous exhaustion. Improvising this conversation will help to establish a clear picture of how and why Celia had to fight, and with whom, to be allowed to return. Including members of the male teaching staff in the improvisation injects even more potential for conflicting views; indeed, an actor may also find that this improvisation helps to inform the opposition to women's education that Radleigh expresses to Mr Banks at the end of Act Two, Scene One ('An Offer').

Improvisation Outline

Time: Spring 1896.

Place: Mrs Welsh's office at Girton.

Characters: Celia, Mrs Welsh, Professor Radleigh, Professor Collins.

Given circumstances: Girton's examination board is meeting to discuss Celia, who has failed her first-year examinations. Mrs Welsh knows that Celia's poor performance was because she had exhausted herself by working so hard. Celia has been asked to come to Mrs Welsh's office so that they can tell her whether she will be allowed to stay at Girton or not.

Scene Six: Raising the Banner

Carolyn and Tess are buying fabric from Mrs Lindley's haberdashery in Cambridge when Lloyd and Edwards enter. The women are planning to make a banner for the graduation campaign. Edwards asks why he has not seen them around, and the women reply that since Dr Maudsley had them banned they have had to take lectures at their college. Meanwhile, Holmes comes to take delivery of a pair of gloves from Paris. Suddenly, Lloyd turns on the women. He asks why they are even bothering to campaign when they have no chance of winning. He launches into an angry tirade against them, comparing his own superior education to theirs and ridiculing the idea that they deserve to study at a place as prestigious as Cambridge. He says that they are unnatural, as no real woman would give up the chance to be a wife or a mother purely for an education. Carolyn tries to fight back, but Lloyd calls her a prostitute and the women leave in shocked silence. Lloyd tries to buy a pair of blue stockings. Mrs Lindley refuses to serve Lloyd, but it transpires that his father owns the premises; when Lloyd threatens to tell him, she realises that she might lose her job unless Lloyd gets what he wants.

In rehearsal:

In her rehearsal process, Jessica often uses Actioning, which is a rehearsal technique most notably used by the director Max Stafford-Clark, with whom she worked closely during her time at Out of Joint. Actioning is based on the Stanislavskian concepts of *units* and *objectives*. Scenes are divided into units and within each unit a character has an objective: what they want from the situation, or from another character, in that moment. Once a character's objective has been established, Actioning involves working out what a character is actively doing on every line to achieve that objective. Actions should always be transitive verbs (e.g. active 'doing words') and are directed from the character saying the line to the character they are saying it to (e.g. the direct object). When first working with actions, an actor might speak the relevant transitive verb before each line or sentence, but ultimately each action should be communicated simply by how they deliver the line.

Some directors spend significant time in the rehearsal room breaking down the text and assigning an action to every line; however, the technique can also be used on selected scenes or speeches. Actioning can be particularly useful when working on monologues, as it can help the actor to find variety of tone within a speech and explore alternative ways of delivering lines, while encouraging them to be specific about what each line is trying to achieve. When directing the play at RADA, Jessica used Actioning to rehearse Lloyd's monologue. The following is an example of what actions might be used for the start of the speech (pp. 88–9).

LLOYD. Listen!

Lloyd's outburst interrupts Carolyn. With this line he is trying to make her be quiet, and therefore '*silences*' is the action chosen.

I was at school at five.

Lloyd is telling the women about himself in order to make the women appreciate his superior education. It is possible to use the action *'informs'*; however, there might be a more interesting choice. The action *'tutors'* perhaps better communicates Lloyd's patronising attitude to the women.

> At seven I knew Plato.

Lloyd is showing off, and *'impresses'* turns that into a playable action that he can actively try to do to the other character.

> At twelve, hand me a cadaver and I'd tell you the name of every last nerve in it.

Carolyn and Tess will already know that Lloyd has had a superior education to them, so Lloyd is not exactly telling them anything new. Instead, Lloyd might be trying to *'overwhelm'* the women with examples of his prowess. Although that could be used, sometimes a more vivid word is easier for an actor to translate into their performance; *'bombards'* suggests a violent and relentless attack so might make for a more dynamic choice.

> You think you can compete?

Lloyd then changes tactic and turns the focus from the quality of his own education, to that of the women. He asks them an outright question, which might suggest he *'quizzes'*, but that feels too gentle; *'challenges'* is perhaps a better reflection of his hostile tone.

> You think some tuppenny once-a-week governess is enough, do you?

Lloyd compares the schooling that the women have received to his own. The language he uses shows how little he rates it, so he *'mocks'* the women.

> Some tattered notes from your brother?

Actors often respond well to actions that inspire a vivid mental picture of what the character is trying to do, so actions do not have to be entirely literal. With this line Lloyd is putting the women down, so perhaps he *'squashes'* them.

> Some village-dunce school for girls?

Again, he is making fun of the women. It is generally a good idea to try to find a new action for each thought, so as we have already used '*mocks*', '*patronises*' is perhaps more appropriate.

On a first reading, the thoughts at the start of Lloyd's monologue follow a pattern and are relatively similar to one another; however, if that is the case, why does he even bother to keep saying everything he does? Actioning challenges the actor to find a distinct purpose for each and every line. It demonstrates how variety can be found in a monologue and also reminds actors to play different tactics on each line in order to achieve their objectives.

Scene Seven: An Emergency Summit

Mr Banks and Miss Blake meet in a tea room. He warns her that those opposed to the women's right to graduate are gaining in strength and numbers. The two are desperate and powerless to fight back. Mr Banks has been sacked from Trinity because of his support of the women, and Miss Blake has been forced to resign from her teaching position at Girton because of her support for the suffragists. A lady who has overheard their conversation stops by the table and there is a glimmer of hope when they think she might support their campaign, but instead she chastises them for their impropriety and expresses the hope that they lose.

In rehearsal:

Improvisation can explore how characters behave in different locations and circumstances. In the play we do not see what Mr Banks is like at home or with his family, but in this scene we do get a glimpse of his wife's attitude to him having lost his job. That information will create many questions for the actor playing Mr Banks, such as what his wife thinks about Girton and what hopes they have for their own daughters' education, which this improvisation might begin to explore.

Improvisation Outline

Time: The evening after Mr Banks has been offered the Trinity fellowship.

Place: The front room of Mr Banks's home in Cambridge.

Characters: Mr Banks, plus other actors to play his wife, Rose, and daughters.

Given circumstances: Mr Banks arrives home from work and is greeted by his family. Rose knows that he was due to have a meeting at Trinity, but when he left in the morning neither of them knew what it was about. His daughters have been attending their own lessons and are keen to show their father what they have learned.

Scene Eight: King of Hearts

It is evening in the common room at Trinity College, and the male students are getting rowdy. Holmes deals cards as Lloyd pours brandy, although Edwards has already drunk too much. Will is looking for Ralph, who he wants to talk to about Tess, but is instead persuaded to join their drinking game. The men play cards and it is not a coincidence that Edwards loses every round. When he finally faces a forfeit, instead of finishing the bottle he stands and sings a beautiful ballad, much to the surprise of his friends. The men tease Ralph about his love life. He enthusiastically declares that he is in love with a bluestocking, and to prove it to them he pulls out an engagement ring. The men propose a toast to Ralph's beloved, who he tells them is a Newnham student called Eliza. When they ask what happened to Tess, Ralph brushes them off. Will tells Ralph that he had come to speak to him on behalf of his friend Tess, who knows nothing of Ralph's other woman. Ralph apologises and explains that Girton is too political to be accepted by his family, who have high expectations of him.

In rehearsal:

When directing the play at RADA, Jessica wanted to encourage the actors to find the playfulness of this scene. She used this exercise to free the actors from the text and to find a physical way of understanding the dynamic between the men. This exercise is great fun for actors of all ages and is most useful when they have a sense of the structure of the scene. It will take some time to work through; although the warm-up exercise will get actors in the right frame of mind, when working with a confident cast you might choose to skip it and simply try the scene using a range of different animal personas.

Animals

Warm-up

Ask the actors to walk naturally and freely around the room. Tell them that this is Level 1.

Explain that you are going to call out different animals and that, when you do so, the actors should fully become that animal as they continue to move around the room.

Encourage them to use their voices and bodies when being the animal. They should think about how the animal moves, the speed at which it moves, which part of its body leads, where its centre of gravity lies, how its sounds are formed, how it interacts with others like it, and so on.

Call out an animal. When the actors have started imitating the animal fully, tell them that is Level 10.

Remind them that their human state is Level 1. Explain that you are going to call out different numbers and that the strength with which they pretend to be an animal should be guided by the number: for example, 8 will still be clearly the animal, with some human characteristics creeping in; 5 is halfway between human and animal; at 3 they will be essentially back to normal but showing some animal characteristics.

Call out different numbers. They do not have to follow a linear pattern, but the actors will find it easier if there are not massive leaps.

Eventually, get them back to a state of Level 2 or 3. Encourage them to still be precise with which of the animal's characteristics they keep, even when they are almost back to normal.

Repeat the process with different animals. The possibilities are endless, but for this scene animals that might be useful include pigs, peacocks, puppies, gorillas and stags.

Scene Work

Discuss which animal the actors feel best suits the situation and characters in the scene. At RADA, Jessica and the actors decided that gorillas were the best match.

Explain that the same rules as before still apply: Level 1 is fully human, Level 10 is fully animal.

Tell the actors that they are going to improvise the scene as your chosen animal. Stress that they do not have to get every action or word perfect, but should use the structure of the scene to hit the key incidents. Try to use some of the scenic furniture if possible, ensuring it is safe, stable and secure for the actors to use in unexpected ways.

When the actors begin, they might throw themselves into it, ooh-ing and aah-ing, jumping and banging on furniture, or scratching themselves just like gorillas. Great! If they are more hesitant, remind them of how they moved and behaved before at Level 10, and encourage them to apply that level of energy to the scene.

Try the improvisation again at different levels: at Level 5, the scene might be a mixture of speech and grunts; by Level 2 or 3 they will be speaking dialogue, with the odd gorilla behaviour creeping in.

Finally, return to the text and run the scene while encouraging the actors to keep the energy and playfulness of the improvisation.

Jessica's Reflections on 'King of Hearts'

It's really important for the actor playing Ralph to know that he's putting up a front in this scene. He didn't want to break up with Tess, but he's expected to marry someone else. The short section between Ralph and Will at the end is the opportunity to make this clear. Ralph wants to say that he would have loved to be with Tess, but he cannot articulate that because it is too hard. He is also bluffing when he stands and talks about buying a ring. At the Globe we played the group of boys on the main stage, and then for their private conversation the actors playing Ralph and Will came out on to the spit (the extended walkway), which meant that they played the last few lines in the middle of the auditorium, twenty feet from the stage. This helped to make it clear that Ralph needs to be private in his conversation with Will. It also gave us a chance to see Ralph alone, dealing with his disappointment and his frustration, before heading back inside to join 'the gang'.

Scene Nine: Broken Hearts

Will finds Tess reading in the orchard. She is delighted that Will has spoken to Ralph, but angry when he says that Ralph is not suitable for her. The only way for Will to make her understand why he does not approve is to tell her that Ralph has met someone else whom he plans to marry. Tess is shocked and heartbroken. Celia comes to warn her that Miss Bott is looking for them and tells Will to leave. Devastated, Tess resolves to pack up her things and leave Cambridge. She remembers a girl she used to know who did not share her thirst for knowledge, and she is jealous of the simpler life that girl will lead. Ralph has broken her heart and she does not know how to carry on, but Celia reminds her how hard she has worked to get this far and urges her not to throw it all away.

In rehearsal:

This scene is about conflict and resolution, and about confrontation and avoidance. The characters have a push–pull relationship: at any one point one is trying to approach or help the other, who in turn is avoiding them. They are attracted or repelled – like magnets – by what the other is saying. This exercise explores the fact that all three characters in this scene have moments of evading another character, although they also make emotional declarations. When they decide to be honest and stop evading, we hear some of the most heart-wrenching speeches of the play.

Magnets

Ask one actor (Tess) to stand in a ring of cast members, who hold hands to create a moveable circular wall. The other actor (Will, then Celia) will stand outside the ring.

Now play the scene. The outside actor (Will or Celia) must try and get to Tess through the circle. They can talk through the circle, move round it, try and break into it, crawl under it. Tess must decide when to engage, when to use the circle to protect her, when to stay within its confines, when to meet the other actor, or even when to leave the circle.

There will also be points when Will or Celia want to avoid Tess; might they then move away from the circle, cross to the other side, or duck away?

Play with the dynamics of the scene and find variety in order to avoid the trap of each actor solely using persuasive tones, when there are lots of other tactics available.

Scene Ten: The Viva

The women are undertaking their viva voce examinations (an oral examination based on a written thesis, where the student is interrogated by an examination board in person about their work). They are being examined by Collins, Radleigh and Mrs Welsh. Celia has written about a young scientist in Switzerland called Albert Einstein, who is challenging the received wisdom of Galileo and Isaac Newton. Carolyn has developed a formula to chart the movement of icebergs, which might protect ships on transatlantic crossings. Tess has found a new way of measuring and classifying stars. However, when she is asked about Cuvier, whose work she never got round to revising, Tess struggles to respond. Celia and Carolyn are awarded passes, but Radleigh tells Tess that she has failed to achieve excellence across all disciplines and therefore cannot pass. Mrs Welsh tells Tess that she will have to go home. Just as the women take in Tess's failure, Mrs Welsh surprises them by saying that she will make an exception and allow her to return to Girton for the new term. Tess promises not to let Mrs Welsh down, and the women celebrate.

In rehearsal:

This scene is dense with scientific arguments and information. In the Globe production, the director John Dove made the exchanges dazzlingly quick-fire to communicate the scope of the women's intellects. To achieve such an effect, the audience must feel that the characters are in complete command of the material, even if they themselves have lost the thread of the argument. Any physical exercise outlined elsewhere in the book will help to create this energy; however, an alternative approach is to play the scene without the actors looking at one another. This will help actors to focus on listening and communicating with each other, and because they have their backs to everyone else, they have to work much harder to capture the others' attention with what they are saying.

Radio Play

Set up the room so that the actors cannot see each other, either by having them sit in a blackout or by getting them to stand in a circle facing outwards with their backs to the centre.

Ask the actors to run the lines of the scene without looking at who they are speaking to.

Encourage them to project the energy of what they are saying out into the room in order to capture everyone's attention, rather than it feeling as though they are just talking to someone opposite them.

Scene Eleven: Voting Day

Girton is decked out with banners as the vote on whether to allow the women the right to graduate is held in Cambridge. Mrs Welsh rallies the women with a speech, although none of them are happy that they are not also being given a say. Will arrives, agitated, and suggests that the gates be shut and that Mrs Welsh does not go outside. The town centre is in chaos and a crowd of angry men are heading towards Girton after having vandalised other colleges. What is more, they have burned an effigy of a woman wearing blue stockings in the town square. Mrs Welsh defies his warning and heads outside. As she does so, windows are broken and a crowd of men led by Lloyd and Holmes force themselves into Girton. A riot ensues as the men pull the banners down, Lloyd and Will get into a fight and Mr Banks gets punched. Mrs Welsh returns and sees the damage. Furious, she runs at Lloyd who throws her to the ground. Everyone stands in shocked silence when Mr Peck comes in and announces that the women have lost the vote. Mrs Welsh is devastated, so Mr Banks helps her. Lloyd leaves, and Holmes and Edwards apologise to the women and ask what they will do now that they have no chance of being allowed to graduate. Tess replies resolutely that it does not matter and that they will carry on.

In rehearsal:

When the rioters attack Girton, they are attacking something that the women have worked hard to create. This improvisation will give the actors a greater feeling of investment in their surroundings, and will therefore make the sight of its destruction even more potent. It will work best if the actors can use at least some of the set and props (or good substitutes). The more options they are given, the more likely they are to come up with new ways of doing things or with moments of business that the design team can then respond to. By the end, you might even decide to incorporate the improvisation into the set-change at the start of the scene, which was how it started at RADA.

Improvisation Outline

Time: The morning of the day of the vote.

Place: The entrance hall of Girton College.

Characters: Tess, Carolyn, Celia, Mrs Welsh, Mr Banks, Minnie, Mr Peck.

Given circumstances: The Girton staff and students are decorating the entrance hall in anticipation of a victory celebration if the vote goes their way. There is lots to be done: moving the furniture to make space for people, deciding where the two large banners are going to be hung and fixing them there, decorating the room, tidying away students' notes and books, and preparing food and drink for the supporters.

Scene Twelve: If You Had to Choose

Will is about to board a train to leave Cambridge for the summer holidays. Tess, who is out of breath from having run to catch him, calls out to stop him. She remembers when Miss Blake asked her to choose between love and knowledge. She knows now that she could never choose love over knowledge, but although her heart has been broken by Ralph, she hopes that in time she might love again. Will says that he will wait for her, even when she is off charting the stars in the southern hemisphere, as they will both be back in Cambridge next September. As Tess and Will embrace, the Girton anthem is sung and the audience are informed that it took fifty years for Cambridge to award women the right to graduate.

In rehearsal:

Proximity is an interesting dynamic to explore in this scene because Will and Tess's relationship has been tested throughout the play, and their sense of ease around each other might not have recovered, despite their strong feelings. This exercise uses the practice of feeding-in to strip the actors of dialogue and instead ask them to communicate purely through movement and positioning. The aim is to reflect the emotional arc of the scene through a continuous sequence of movements, with the actors reacting to one another. By the end of an extended period of enforced silence the actors might well be desperate to talk to each other, and directors might choose to recall that sense of urgency when it comes to rehearsing the scene, as well as remaining alert to interesting spatial dynamics that might emerge during the exercise.

Silent Waltz

Get the actors playing Will and Tess to stand at opposite ends of the space and maintain eye contact.

Assign each actor a 'feeder', who will read in the dialogue from the sidelines. Again, the lines should be fed thought by thought, which is likely to be sentence by sentence. In this exercise, the actors do not speak the lines that they have been fed but instead use them to motivate a physical movement in the space.

As each new thought is spoken, the actors should move closer together or further apart depending on the feeling behind the line. It is important that actors do not stop and think between being fed the line and moving, and instead trust their instincts.

The lines should be fed neutrally, at a steady pace and without stress or intonation, but the feeders need to be sensitive to the speed with which the actors are moving so that the lines and movements flow smoothly on from each other.

Once they have got the hang of it, repeat the exercise so that the actors move not only on their own lines, but in response and reaction to each other's lines and movements. Remind them that the only thing with which they have to communicate the full force of their character's emotion is their body in relation to the other person's.

At first the moves may be quite tentative or naturalistic as the actors try to recreate the scene in a literal manner. But as the actors get more confident with the exercise, repeat it and encourage them to explore a full range of movement, and to make them more expressive. Some thoughts might draw them tight together and others might push them to the furthest ends of the room; some moves might be small, quick and impulsive, and others large, slow and deliberate.

*

A Note on Scene Titles

Not all playwrights title each scene in the way that Jessica has chosen to do in *Blue Stockings*. How, then, might the titles serve not merely as a route through the text, but as a way to inform actors and audiences about the deeper meanings of each scene?

In Brecht's theatre, scene titles are frequently shared with the audience to alert them to what they are about to see. Thus, 'The Laws of Motion' refers to Isaac Newton's three laws, the subject of Mr Banks's lesson, but also serves as a metaphor for the women's own progress and the ultimately unstoppable force of their campaign. Likewise, 'The Garden of Eden' hints at something to come: the biblical Garden of Eden is paradise and home to Adam and Eve before the fall of mankind, so the reference to it at Ralph and Tess's first meeting warns us that their bliss will not last.

The titles can also comment on the play's deeper themes and arguments. The phrase 'Bread and Circuses' was initially coined by the poet Juvenal in Ancient Rome. It implies that all the people want is to have their basic needs satisfied and to be entertained, which will distract them from their forgotten civic duty of political engagement. In the play, the term is used ironically because, of course, Carolyn is actively trying to engage politically by going to hear Millicent Fawcett speak. Yet it also hints at an idea held by some that certain rights or concessions might be offered to women (in place of the 'bread and circuses') to keep them placated – others argued that those would mean nothing unless women could fully engage in all aspects of political life. Indeed, that strikes at the heart of the debate between Miss Blake and Mrs Welsh over the tension between the women's education and their political engagement, with the unresolved question of which is more important to women's overall advancement.

Likewise, 'Raising the Banner' is both a literal reference to what the women are planning to do with the 'forty yards of calico' they are buying from Mrs Lindley (p. 86) and a rallying cry with echoes of the biblical injunction 'Lift ye up a banner upon the high mountain' (Isaiah 13:2).[16] For millenia, the concept of raising a banner has had strong military connotations, as forces raise standards to act as a rallying point for troops. Not only does Lloyd's anger in the scene foreshadow the violent confrontation of the riot itself, but the women raising a banner (at the summit of the 'Girton grind' no less) symbolises them rallying others to their cause – indeed, to their fight.

Scene Timeline

The action of the play spans the course of an academic year (September to June), but because there are a lot of scenes in an episodic format it can be helpful for actors to understand how recently major events happened and what time has passed between scenes.

When directing the play at RADA, Jessica set the cast the task of creating a timeline. Each scene title was written on a separate piece of paper, which the cast then collaboratively laid out along the length of the rehearsal room floor, using clues in the script and their own research as a guide. The titles were placed at varying distances from one another, with the distances between them roughly illustrating the length of time that passed between each scene. Jessica and the cast then walked and talked the play through from start to finish, discussing what had happened in the periods of time in between scenes and adjusting the timeline when necessary.

This timeline should serve as a guide for a similar exercise. Scenes that happen on the same day have been grouped together, with suggestions given for dates and time scales that the script does not make explicit. Casts might come up with slightly different choices for some of the time scales, depending on their research or interpretation of the text, but once the timeline has been agreed by everyone, it can be transferred on to a wall in the rehearsal room for all to refer to.

Act One
September 1896

The first day of term
Prologue: The students arrive
at Cambridge.

The second day of term
The Laws of Motion: The
Girton students have their
first lesson with Mr Banks.
Sightseeing: The men spot
Tess riding a bicycle.

**During the first week of
term**
The Happiness Equation: The
Girton students have their
first lesson with Miss Blake.

**In the middle of the
term, on the same day**
The Wandering Womb: Dr
Maudsley gives a lecture.
Out Without Hats: Tess and
Will meet in the street.
Fragments of the World: Mrs
Welsh talks to Tess about her
behaviour in Dr Maudsley's
lecture.

Later that week
The Dictionary: Ralph and
Tess meet in the library.

A few days later
The Great Escape: After Will
comes to visit, Tess sneaks
out to see Ralph.
The Garden of Eden: Ralph
and Tess meet in the
orchard.

**In the second half of the
term**
The Merits of Moral Science:
The Girton students show
Miss Blake how far they have
come.

**Towards the end of the
term**
An Arrival: Billy arrives at
Girton to take Maeve home.

The next day
Science of the Heart: Mr
Banks gives the male
students Tess's essay.
An Education: Mrs Welsh
addresses the Senate as
Maeve leaves Girton.

December 1896

Act Two
January 1897

Before term starts
An Offer: Mr Banks is
offered a job at Trinity.

The first week of term
The Telescope: The Girton
students are reunited after
Christmas. Will confesses his
feelings for Tess.
Time Travellers: Ralph and
Tess go stargazing.

**Saturday, at the end of
the first week of term**
Bread and Circuses: Mrs
Welsh catches Carolyn
sneaking out and gives Miss
Blake an ultimatum.

In the middle of the term
Outcasts: Celia finds Tess
thinking about Ralph, when
she should be revising.

**The weeks preceding the
vote, during Spring term**
Raising the Banner: Carolyn
and Tess shop for material to
make a banner.

**The weeks preceding the
vote, during Spring term**
An Emergency Summit: Miss
Blake and Mr Banks discuss
how the campaign is going.

**May 1897, on the same
day**
King of Hearts: Will goes to
speak to Ralph about Tess.
Broken Hearts: Tess is
heartbroken when Will tells
her Ralph has met someone
else.

The next morning
The Viva: The Girton
students are examined.

The next day
Voting Day: Cambridge votes
on whether the women should
be allowed to graduate.

The end of term
If You Had to Choose: Tess
finds Will before he leaves
for the summer.

June 1897

Playing the Part

Although every actor and director will bring their own ideas and interpretation to a production, being aware of the play's modern context is important because the period setting of *Blue Stockings* can suggest an acting style that does it no favours. Audiences tend to be used to modern plays being set in the present and period plays being set in the past, so it is relatively unusual to have a modern play by a young writer that is set over a hundred years ago. That should not, however, lead actors and directors to think that *Blue Stockings* has to be played the same as they would a late-Victorian play. Indeed, Jessica says that 'the big trap actors and directors should avoid is making the play stuffy and starchy' by using heightened received pronunciation or moving in a physically restricted way.

CHARACTERISATION

For any actor or director embarking on a production of *Blue Stockings*, the playwright's 'Note to the Players' is a good place to start (pp. 7–8). Jessica uses it to outline her interpretation of the male and female characters, which is expanded on below.

A fun way to start thinking about character in rehearsal is to ask the actors to cast *Blue Stockings: The Movie*. Which well-known actors would they pick and why? Who would they choose to play their character? What traits might those actors bring to the role? Get them to think about which actor would be their first choice, and also to pick a wild card – someone surprising who might bring something different to the role. Ask them to keep this in mind when they return to their performances, in order to find different colours in the playing.

The Women

Although 'we tend to associate the Victorian era with stuffiness, modesty and proper manners' (p. 7), Jessica's advice is that the female characters should be played as modern women who just happen to wear corsets, which they can't wait to get rid of in order to wear trousers instead! There's always a temptation for actors to play the female leads as a bit too fey, a bit too girly – and soft and sweet with it. But in the scenes between Tess and Will, for example, she is telling him how it is, and if she is played like a Victorian woman in a 'victim scenario', that would really discredit her and what a sparky individual she is.

It is interesting to consider whether girls in the late-nineteenth century were inherently different from girls today. Jessica does not think that they were 'born as softer, quieter creatures than now. We are exactly the same; it's just that there were different social expectations. Actors need to remember that these girls have defied all expectations in order to get here. They are already the sparkiest, quickest, most intelligent, witty girls in the country and they need to be played like that.' Jessica likens them to 'all the sparky heroines of the past: Maid Marian, Lizzie Bennet, Marianne Dashwood.[17] That is what we should be thinking about, and not willowy Victorian heroines who faint.'

Yet, the play's director at Shakespeare's Globe, John Dove, cautions that avoiding the corset trap and thinking of them as modern women should not mean losing sight that they 'were in a strictly coded Victorian world'. He says that keeping those restrictions in mind makes their achievements even more remarkable. 'It is amazing that they managed to do what they did. They were fighting against it, but they did not know where that fight was going to take them because they did not have a map.' Likewise, Verity Kirk, who played Gertie/Tess in the RADA production, recognises that the women's strength should not alienate their audience. 'At the beginning I felt like she is feisty in the way that I am feisty,'

Verity says, 'but I needed to rein it in, otherwise she became too strident and too pushy to be a heroine that the audience find identifiable.'

The Men

It can be easy for actors to play some of the male characters as ogres, but it is vital that every actor believes in what their character is saying. Jessica says that 'if an actor tries to play someone as an evil bastard, the audience are never going to believe it. The truth about the men in this play is that they were real people and they felt these feelings, which we now find quite difficult to swallow, for very good reasons.'

John Dove agrees that, 'fundamentally, the key is not to let all the men be villains', and, 'like any play', he achieved this in the Globe production, 'by bringing out the humanity'. He says that it is important for actors to understand the historical context in order to appreciate where the men's perspectives stem from, because 'the idea of a woman having a degree was bewildering for a lot of men'.

Occasionally the play finds the male students in awkward situations, and because they are usually so capable and quick-witted it can be very enjoyable to see them floundering. Such moments tend to revolve around encounters with women, as when Edwards is confronted by Miss Bott in Dr Maudsley's lecture, or Ralph tries to woo Tess in the orchard. It is helpful to remember that, in this era, men from their social backgrounds were likely to have had little experience dealing with women. Unless they had sisters, boys who went to boarding school would simply not have encountered women like those at Girton before, which explains why they are not as confident around them as they are with their studies.

THE ACTOR'S BODY

The body is not only an actor's tool, it is also the prime indicator of class, status and character, and in the 1890s, status was everything. An actor should think carefully about how to use their body in performance, to reveal who their character is, where they are from and what their attitudes are.

Although *Blue Stockings* has the spirit of a modern play, it is vital that in performance the actors move in a way that conveys the truth of the era. Physicality tells us an enormous amount about both social expectations and training, and a character's personality. At RADA the cast worked with both Senior Movement Director Francine Watson Coleman and the movement tutor Katya Benjamin to find the appropriate physicality. It was impressed on them from the beginning that, in order to get a character right, they had to get the body right first.

Background

The body and how we use it has always been an indicator of status. Since Graeco-Roman times, deportment (learning how to hold yourself and move) has been evidence of an intellectual approach to the body. People with money and leisure time have had the luxury to learn desirable physical habits and care about how they come across physically. They are trained to sit, stand and move in a particular way, which tells others that they are people of class – the elite. The body, therefore, tells those around you about your social status before you even speak.

In simple terms, people brought up with money and education (city folk, the upper and upper-middle classes) have been taught how to move; people without money (country people, the working class) have not. The latter conducted themselves differently, in a manner that was perceived to be untrained, uneducated, naive. For many years this helped people distinguish the rich from the poor, both in real life and on stage.

However, over time, the importance of learning correct deportment has eroded. Clothes, which originally contorted people into particular shapes (think about the extreme shapes of Restoration dresses cut to hoist women into a particular figure and posture), have become increasingly easy to wear. In Shakespeare's time it took a great deal of effort to dress, as women would have been laced into dresses with corsets and boning; but by the end of the 1800s the silhouettes had simplified, and women had less bulk to cope with. Today, there is no formal posture training and we could not be expected to tell how much someone has in their bank account simply by looking at their posture. That indicates the deformalisation of society and a more relaxed attitude to social class.

The Body in the Late Victorian Era

At the time the play is set, deportment was still a key social skill. At the end of the 1800s, the expectation for both women and men was to be elegant and refined. Dance styles can often tell us a good deal about how people moved in their everyday lives, so think about the types of dance that were popular. This era is pre-jazz and pre-American popular music, and dance styles were formal and elevated (amongst the upper and middle classes anyway, which are the general focus of the play).

Formality was an expectation, but the end of the Victorian era was a time of change. Bowing and curtsying were out and the handshake was just beginning. Etiquette books were widely available, so although some of the characters may not have been tutored specifically in how to move, they would have come across these books and would be au fait with the techniques. Some of the characters might be more attached to the old, more formal ways, while others might be throwing caution to the wind and embracing a new, less formal manner. For example, Carolyn has spent time with radicals and bohemians on her travels, so although she is arguably the poshest of the girls, she is also the kind to abandon her corset, as some very modern women were then doing. However, Carolyn is still a Victorian; she has had a base level of formality ingrained in her from childhood, so even if she is more relaxed, she is still a woman of her time and not ours.

Although women may not have been quite as constrained by bustles and martingales as they had been in previous eras, they were still restrained by the single element of clothing that tells you everything you need to know about society's attitude to women: the corset. They were held in, pulled up and restricted; however, there is a common misconception that corset-wearing automatically means 'stiff'. It doesn't. In fact, when a woman had been appropriately trained in the art of wearing a corset (if her family was posh enough), she would have been absolutely at ease.

Being at Ease

The trick to playing someone comfortable with their social class is that they look effortless. They sit straight, but with ease. They hold themselves beautifully, but with ease. They never appear outwardly uncomfortable because they were, supposedly, born elegant, so it is easy for them to be naturally upright. Anyone sitting stiffly clearly has not been brought up well enough to know how to sit properly; they are likely to be a try-hard or an imposter. Really 'classy' people never try hard. Think containment, grace, equilibrium, and ease not effort; it is all about how you are seen.

Ease of posture can help distinguish between characters. Maeve would not have had the sort of upbringing where she was taught how to stand. So perhaps she tries to copy the others and attempts to be upright but is too stiff, rather than at ease. Or perhaps she feels comfortable enough to stand naturally the way she always has done, in which case she might slouch and be looked down on by those 'in the know'.

The men in *Blue Stockings* are educated and therefore expected to behave as polite, respectable gentlemen. They would have been trained from a young age to stand with good posture, to sit and move with ease, and to maintain a degree of formality. They must not seem like twenty-first-century guys; they are far more poised than that.

Exercises for 1890s Posture

The Right Clothes

The easiest way to start on the path towards better posture is to work with the right costume to get comfortable and used to the new way of moving, which needs to become second nature. Women should rehearse in corsets and shoes with a low heel; likewise, men should wear the appropriate formal shoes. It is almost impossible to move like a Victorian if rehearsing in trainers!

Learning to Conduct Yourself With Ease

Try sitting down. Sit upright to look confident and at ease with yourself. Do not slouch, sit back in the chair or cross your legs. Sit on your sitting bones and keep your spine comfortably elevated, not rigid. It is harder than it sounds.

Now, try moving. Remember, classy people do not hurry; hurrying is what the working class do. The characters' minds are quick, but their bodies should not be allowed to overtake, and you should therefore always feel in control physically. Do not rush. Move quickly, but remember: you are still at ease. To be at ease is supremely fashionable.

Look at your steps. Each step should not be more than the length of a long foot. Women, in particular, should control the size of their stride. Keep upright, let your shoulders sit back, and glide.

Think about how much social training your character has had and adapt your walk and seat accordingly. There would be a base level of formality whatever your social background, especially somewhere like Cambridge, so no character should move like a person from the twenty-first century; but experiment with degrees of formality and ease to find the right level for your character.

Wearing a Corset

A corset should not be a means of keeping you upright – you ought to be upright and at ease anyway – but it should rather give shape by slimming the waist and lifting the chest.

First, put the corsets on. You will have to work with a partner and do each other's up because you cannot do it yourself (this is why servants are useful when you are a Victorian!).

Stand with your weight evenly placed on each foot. Do not splay the feet, but have them pointing forward. Drop your sternum. Lift up through the back. Make sure you do not fall forward into the corset. Instead, keep the head up and lift, bringing the energy up to the head. Project it up and out. Feel the tone and muscularity that this gives you in the front of your legs. Allow the lift to extend throughout your upper body. Now allow the weight to move into the balls of the feet. Do not rock backwards. Keep the weight out of your heels – this way you keep forward and present yourself as switched-on and curious, gently alert. A corset is about lift and elegance, so enjoy it. Try to sit like this and then walk, remembering the lessons above.

At RADA, our movement coach Francine said that ladies should think of themselves as 'standing on a single pin, not on a box'. In other words, stay dainty, stay poised and do not let your weight drop into the floor.

Male Posture

Stand up with alertness. Now pull up through the thighs and allow this light tension to travel up through the pelvis and the lower back, thereby giving you an elegant lift without stiffening. Do not stiffen your back; allow the poise to come from the legs.

Keep at least one leg straight whenever you stand. Do not splay the feet, but have them facing forward. Now lift up and allow the head to sit comfortably and proudly, with shoulders set back a little. The head is the seat of consciousness, so you need to use lift in the upper body to allow the head to lead. This will help you look and feel more intellectual.

Gentlemen did not cross their arms because it was considered rude. Allow the hands to sit comfortably, either to the side or behind the back. Remember, you should be formal but at ease.

Try moving around the space using these techniques, then apply them in a scene.

Energy and Stakes

Good drama is about conflict. For each character, that conflict lies in what they want and what obstacles stand in the way of them getting it. Every character in *Blue Stockings* wants something, although that might change over the course of the play; love, getting good grades, keeping women out of Cambridge, and winning the right to graduate, are just a few examples, but actors will always identify more. If actors keep their character's goal, or objective, in mind, it will help them to play each scene with energy and will also remind them what is at stake.

What is more, these characters never give up. Even at the end of the play none of them have achieved entirely what they want: Mrs Welsh's campaign for the vote may have failed, but the Girton women still vow to carry on and defy those who would rather see them gone. Once the female students' eyes have been opened to what their lives could be like, their expectations constantly expand. John Dove characterises this as 'the predicament of an Olympic athlete – once you get to Olympic level, you can see that there is more, so you go for more and then the horizon moves on again. In that sense, they do not achieve an accomplishment, because there is always another one beyond it.'

The pace and comedy of the text helps actors to maintain that energy. Actress Verity Kirk remembers the snappy dialogue meaning that she was 'constantly bouncing off other people'. For her, maintaining the character's energy was 'about picking up on one another and remembering that they are all incredibly intelligent', and she likens the dialogue to 'watching politicians talk to one another and realising they are decrypting and thinking in a different way to us. They listen, and then they are quick to respond because they are smart people who have already thought about their response.'

IMPROVISATION

In rehearsal, Jessica finds it helpful to explore the exterior circumstances of the play, such as family background or the politics of the time, and to do improvisations around scenes, rather than improvise the specific events of the play. She will often set up an improvisation scenario by supplying the actors with the given circumstances. For example, if they were improvising Carolyn finding out that she has got in to Cambridge, Jessica would say: 'This is New Year's Eve in Paris. Carolyn is an only child and the five other characters in the scene are Carolyn's mum, dad, aunt, a famous psychiatrist and a famous opera singer. The clock is about to strike midnight and there are five minutes to gather drinks before the New Year.'

Sometimes she will set an improvisation up with different groups at the same time. There may be sixteen people in the cast, but for one set of improvisations she might just be exploring the characters of the four Girton students, so she will split the cast into four groups and tell the other actors to play their parents, for example. Each of the groups will go away and improvise their scenario before bringing it back and sharing the choice bits. It can be useful to let people improvise and then choose to show or expand on a section that they find interesting; otherwise you can end up with the whole group watching very long improvisations that do not necessarily go anywhere.

Another way is to share the improvisation immediately and have the director repeatedly stop and start it. In that case,

Jessica might throw in things that mess with the situation. In the same example she might say, 'The doorbell goes,' then pick another actor to play the postman and tell the actors, 'This is Carolyn's letter to say that she has got into Cambridge. Dad knows that she did the entrance exam, but Mum knows nothing about it.' In that case, she is not telling the actors what to think, but is telling them what they do and do not know so that they can respond appropriately. It is useful to do that sort of improvisation just once, because if you repeat it, you can never get the freshness of it again.

Further Improvisation Scenarios

- Maeve leaving home for Girton.
- The women arriving at Girton on their first day, meeting Minnie and finding their rooms.
- Dinner on the first day and Mrs Welsh's welcoming speech.
- The women's first-night 'cocoa party' at Girton.
- Mrs Welsh questioning Mr Banks about the fact the women have been seen out on the front lawn in their bloomers.
- Mr Banks apologising to Dr Maudsley after the debacle in the lecture about hysteria.
- Dr Maudsley at home telling his wife what happened at the lecture.
- Tess confessing to Minnie what happened in the library with Ralph.
- Edwards with Maudie on their trip to the coast.
- Ralph and Tess exchanging Christmas presents.
- Lloyd getting a dressing-down from his father.
- The boys meeting during the holidays at Edwards's house.
- The boys arriving back at Trinity after the holidays.

- Holmes meeting Mr Banks to ask for career advice.
- Miss Blake going to her first suffrage meeting.

Staging Considerations

Having seen a number of different productions of *Blue Stockings*, Jessica feels strongly that there is always more than one way of playing any scene, although some ideas may be more or less appropriate than others. Every director and designer will use their own understanding of the play, the physical demands of the performance space, the resources that are available, and the skills and ideas of the rest of the production team to interpret and bring to life each scene. Nonetheless, there are a number of specific things to consider when staging the play.

DIRECTION

Blue Stockings is written in a relatively filmic way, with a series of short scenes that run into each other. The pace of the play means that the action is like a ball rolling down a hill, getting faster and faster. The action is driven by the question of whether the women are going to win the vote and the right to graduate, and directors should explore ways of maintaining that dynamic. Partly, it can be communicated by the energy that actors start and end each scene with, so that the action builds in intensity; however, design and staging also play a crucial role.

Jessica's primary tip for preserving the play's energy is to keep any scene changes to an absolute minimum. If directors and designers put blackouts and scene changes between every scene it risks slowing the pace down. When Jessica started working at Shakespeare's Globe, the Artistic Director of the time, Dominic Dromgoole, told her that the best way to direct in that space is for one scene to start as soon as the actors in the previous scene have turned their backs. There is no need to wait for actors to get off stage; as soon as they have turned away the next scene can start, because the audience will have changed focus. Applying that tip to *Blue Stockings* means that the energy flows out of one scene and straight into the next. Directors should have faith that the audience are imaginative enough to fill in the gaps and understand where each scene is set without multiple changes of furniture.

Blue Stockings is by no means a fairytale, but there is something slightly elevated about the tone of the play. It is consciously theatrical, which is particularly evident in scenes where there is a nudge to the audience, like when Miss Bott says, 'They must think I was born yesterday' (p. 49). That line can be delivered to herself, but it is often addressed out to the audience. With the fourth wall broken in a moment like that, there becomes no reason to be too precious about keeping every other aspect of the production totally realistic.

SET

The fact that *Blue Stockings* is written in the form of multiple short scenes creates practical challenges for designers to consider. The set needs to be flexible so that it can represent a range of indoor and outdoor locations without the need for cumbersome changes between them. Moreover, *Blue Stockings* requires an unusually large cast for a modern play, and some scenes, such as the riot, require large numbers of actors on stage, which the set will need to accommodate. When designers factor in the potential array of costumes, including hats, that might be used, the result could be quite an overwhelming stage picture.

One of the easiest ways to deal with those challenges is to create a set that is a blank canvas, able to be transformed into lots of different things. There have been beautiful set designs for *Blue Stockings* that have used piles of books, library furniture or big pieces of wood that transformed into trees, bookshelves or pillars. Another way to enable the action to flow swiftly from one scene to the next is to create different playing areas on the stage representing different locations.

It is also helpful for designers to research and consider the architecture of Cambridge and the colleges themselves, and they might employ height as a result. Towering bookcases that dwarf the students might symbolise the weight of history and expectation that surrounds them, and provide opportunities to use ladders to create dynamic stage pictures. Remember, though, that even on a totally bare stage, actors can communicate the scale and grandeur of the buildings that surround them through their expressions and eyelines when they imagine looking around at the view.

The physical location and unique architecture of each and every performance space influences the audience's experience and understanding of drama. Imagine what profound resonance and relevance the play might have if performed at dusk in a garden of a Cambridge college. Jessica feels that there is no space that is inappropriate for this play; it has been performed in the round, in a proscenium theatre and even in the open air. Such spaces always add a specific dynamic. The important thing is that directors and designers respond to the space, explore how it speaks to the themes of the play, and place the audience in such a way that they get the most out of it.

Jason Jamerson's Reflections on the Set

Early on, the director and I decided that smooth, fast transitions were critical to the pacing of the play. Because of this, I wanted to avoid representing every location with heavy, slow scenery. I chose an extremely simple interior: it's only three flat walls with doors in them, unattached upstage for more sweeping entrances and exits.

From the beginning, I wanted the clutter of set dressing to push us into that scientific, yet oddball and sometimes eerie world of late-Victorian academia. Later, the idea of using blackboard paint and filling in the gaps with engravings and mathematical formulae gave us another layer of

The set of *Blue Stockings* at Columbia Preparatory School, New York. Scenic Design by Jason Jamerson (www.jasonjamerson.com).

detail and depth. The clever scene titles we couldn't do without, and so we projected them above the centre door during transitions, which blended right in with our chalk drawings.

All of this, however, was just meant to frame and set the mood for the big open space where the actors do the real storytelling. A table here, and you're in the library. A dress stand there, and you're in the haberdasher's, and the various props provide different-shaped slaloms to keep the blocking dynamic as well.

PROPS AND FURNITURE

Designers should consider whether there is any need to change furniture between scenes instead of simply keeping it on stage. Audiences will readily accept that a chair used in one location can also be used in a different location. For example, one production simply had several armchairs that the teachers used, and one set of chairs that all the students used. Another kept all of the furniture on stage throughout so that in Act One, Scene One ('The Laws of Motion'), Tess had to cycle around the sofas and desks, which made the scene all the more precarious.

If possible, it can be helpful to use some rehearsal time to get the actors to play around inventively with what can be achieved with chairs, tables and pieces of set. What can a stack of books or suitcases become? What can a bookshelf or desk become? One item might serve a lot of purposes. Picture a large oak desk with a green leather top. It might be where Tess writes, while also serving as a library table or an office desk at Girton or Trinity, but if Tess and Ralph stand on it, could it be transformed into a hillside with a slight change in lighting state?

Props can also provide opportunities to tell the story in new and unexpected ways. In the RADA production, Miss Bott spent the entire play knitting blue stockings that the women then wore on voting day. The pride on Miss Bott's face when she saw the students wearing her handiwork spoke volumes about her relationship with them.

Arguably the most powerful item that the audience could see is not specified in the text, but there is no reason why the smouldering effigy of a woman wearing blue stockings should not be brought on stage by the rioters in Act Two, Scene Eleven ('Voting Day'). As Jessica recalls in her Rehearsal Diary, the actors could improvise making the effigy, which will then serve as a powerful visual representation of the brutality of the riot and strength of feeling when brought on stage.

COSTUME

As with props, costume can reveal a great deal about character and is a way to reflect the deeper themes of the play, which is, of course, itself named after a piece of clothing, as Jessica identifies in the Introduction.

The fashions of the late-nineteenth century offer a range of interesting shapes and details. Costume can reveal the different personalities and cultures of the four women, so it is important that a designer understands that they come from vastly different social backgrounds. For example, Carolyn might wear the brightest and most extravagant clothes and have everything personally made for her, whereas there is explicit reference to the fact that Maeve has one grey dress that she wears the whole time. Celia is slightly more reserved than the other women, which might be reflected through a more traditional style of dress, while Tess's love of the outdoors might necessitate a slightly shorter hemline stopping at the feet rather than a skirt with a train.

At this time, women would still have been expected to wear corsets, although the more bohemian among them were starting to experiment with slightly less constraining silhouettes. Hats or straw boaters would have been worn in public, and hair was worn up, often in a bun. Verity Kirk, who played Gertie in the RADA production, described how putting on her costume gave her an insight into how long it would have taken to get ready in the morning: 'You can see why so many women did not want to do anything – they were constrained physically. It would have been easier to sit down all day and just do needlework. I remember tripping over three or four times in the tech. Cambridge would have been a hazard in those kinds of outfits. Think of the "Girton grind"!'

Because they could not graduate, women were not permitted to wear the formal academic dress that the male students and professors wore. The term 'subfusc' refers to the plain, dark suits that students wore under their academic gowns. Even if subfusc is adopted for the male students' formal wear, subtle differences in cut and style can still communicate class and character. We see Holmes buying the most fashionable gloves from Mrs Lindley's haberdashery, but could there be other touches to his costume to show he is a follower of fashion? Moreover, at Trinity College the academic gowns are dark blue, rather than the usual black, which might serve to emphasise Will's status as an outsider.

LIGHTING

Lighting can aid the play's swift changes between time and location. Scenes repeatedly switch from indoor settings, which tend to be suggested using warmer tones, to outdoors, which are typically portrayed using cooler colours. Likewise, the transformation between day and night can be immediately effected by a change in the colour and intensity of lighting states. Using a warm wash, such as straw, along with yellows and oranges can evoke sunshine; adding blues to a cold neutral colour, such as steel, can place a scene during the night.

Lighting can also add architecture to a set, without the need for physical objects. So shafts of light coming on to the stage, as though through a window, could differentiate between the various interior settings, such as Tess's bedroom and Miss Blake's classroom, and provide a focal point for the actors when Tess is plotting to escape and meet Ralph. Aside from its more literal uses, lighting can also create atmosphere. Different qualities or tones of light might create a different mood for the male-dominated scenes in the lecture theatre or Senate, than in the women's classes in Girton.

SOUND AND EFFECTS

Transitions between scenes can be smoothed through the judicious use of music, yet it is important to think about how one or two familiar pieces can ease the audience's way through the story, rather than lots of different music pulling them out of the action. There are times when sound effects are specified to tell the story, but they can also enhance a scene or be used in a more stylised way for effect. The RADA production employed a knitting sound effect for Miss Bott that was played at a comically loud volume in the library during Act One, Scene Seven. Used in that way, the effect gave the scene a nice sense of momentum, as well as being witty.

Music forms a significant part of the end of the play. The script specifies that the actors sing 'Gaudeamus Igitur', a popular university song (sometimes referred to as 'The Gaudie' and properly known as 'De Brevitate Vitae', or 'On the Shortness of Life') that the real Girton students sang during the graduation campaign. The song's original lyrics are in Latin, although a direct English translation, or the more recent English versions, will help a cast to appreciate that it is a rousing and light-hearted satire on university life. It opens with the celebratory line 'Let us rejoice, therefore, while we are young' but quickly acknowledges that the youthful spirit will pass, for death is just around the corner. Subsequent stanzas pay tribute to teachers, to the fraternity and brotherhood of students, and to all 'easy and beautiful' women. It is certainly interesting to consider why the Girton women adopted the song and how they arguably subverted its message in the process. Musical directors may wish to explore the arrangement of voices in the song, as there can be something poignant about the women starting it off, and the men's voices then joining in.

The final song provides the backdrop for the lasting image of the play, which is a block of text explaining what happened after the play's conclusion. It is Jessica's intention that the words are displayed rather than spoken, and that they are left up as the audience leave the theatre. Directors may choose simply to project the words onto a screen or wall; however, not every space will be suitable and not everyone will have access to such technology. In the Globe production, the text was written on big flags that were pulled down from the ceiling. Alternatively, it could be written on the reverse of the banners that already decorate the college, on blackboards wheeled on stage, or on placards held up by the cast.

As with the rest of the play, there are many different and inventive ways to stage the final moments. For directors and designers, discovering and deciding exactly how to do all that is one of the the most exciting parts of the job.

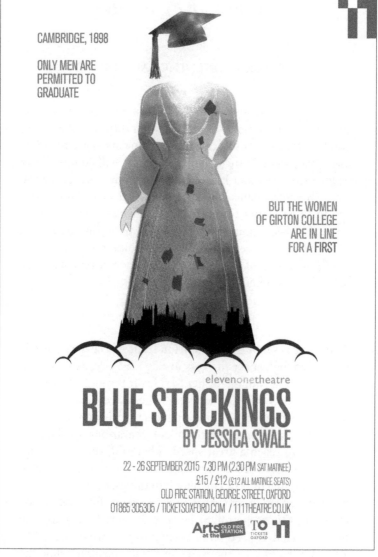

Poster design by Vince Haig (barquing.com) for a production by Eleven One Theatre.

Staging Key Scenes

ACT ONE, SCENE ONE: THE LAWS OF MOTION
Direction

In this scene, the four women meet each other for the first time, so it is important to establish their different characters and first impressions of each other. Allowing space for a few awkward pauses in the opening exchange will communicate Maeve's reserve and her differences from Tess. Likewise, Carolyn might flounce on, talking louder than any of the others and disturbing the formality of Celia's introductions. Once the class begins, the women will be trying to impress Mr Banks, as well as each other, and should find opportunities for moments of unspoken reaction or communion as they listen to each other's answers.

Set

The scene is set outside on Girton College's lawn and needs to have enough space for Tess to ride a bicycle, as well as an exit that is big enough for her to ride off through. Not every theatre is blessed with acres of stage space; however, it is possible to manoeuvre a bike around a surprisingly small area – and Tess's riding is meant to look precarious, so she does not need to reach a great speed. That said, the actress and audience will not feel comfortable if there is a genuine chance of her toppling over or crashing into things, so that risk must be managed. If there is absolutely no room for Tess to ride about in, this scene might be staged safely by placing the bicycle on a disguised set of cycling rollers, which work like a treadmill and keep the frame in a static position while the rider pedals.

Props and Furniture

The women all arrive carrying books, which Mr Banks instructs them to put down when he goes off to collect the bicycle. Bicycles in the late-nineteenth century were far simpler than most of their modern equivalents, with ladies' bikes typically more upright in what we still call a 'sit up and beg' style. It can be difficult and costly to source bicycles of the period, but it is worth doing if at all possible – and there are other scenes in which it can be used to further justify the effort.

Costume

Much is made of the fact that the women appear wearing bloomers. Although some women of the period might have worn bloomer-style trousers as outerwear, the women's reactions and Mr Banks's remarks indicate that these are the split-crotch cotton style that were worn as underwear. A decision needs to be made about how the women are to wear their bloomers and whether they do so in the same way or not. It is possible for the women to still wear their overskirts and petticoats, with the front hems lifted and tucked into the front of their waistbands, revealing the bloomers underneath. Alternatively, they might dispense with skirts entirely and just wear the bloomers over their stockings. The latter is certainly far more risqué, and so perhaps better suited to Carolyn than Celia.

Lighting

At the beginning of the scene the lighting state will change from an interior setting to an exterior one. There does not need to be any change before the following scene because the men are also outdoors.

Sound

The scene ends with the sound of Tess crashing the bicycle offstage. Directors must decide whether to use a recorded sound effect or to have people create the effect live, in which case they can experiment with what combination of items creates the best crashing noise. Either way, the direction that the sound comes from will need to be the same as where Tess rode off, and loud enough to cause the other students alarm.

ACT ONE, SCENE FOUR: THE WANDERING WOMB
Direction

This is one of the busier scenes of the play, with up to ten characters on stage; however, the room it is set in is meant to be even fuller. A lecture by the venerable Dr Maudsley in Cambridge would have been heaving with students and professors, and directors should consider how to create the impression of a crowded lecture hall. One option is to have the audience stand in for other attendees at the lecture, perhaps by seating the male students amongst them or having Dr Maudsley addressing the audience as a whole. Directors should also consider whether the male and female students are seated together or separately, and what might add to the feeling of the women being out of place. It is important, however, that we know Dr Maudsley can see that Tess's arm is raised and is therefore deliberately not inviting her to answer.

Set

The scene is set in a lecture theatre, and it might make sense for Dr Maudsley's positioning to echo where he stood to deliver the prologue. Sightlines are particularly challenging in this scene, as it is important the audience see Dr Maudsley as well as the reactions of the students watching him. Using a raised level or podium might assist, while a more stylised option would be to position all the students behind Dr Maudsley so that his back is to them. All the actors will look and speak straight out to the audience, who will soon realise that they should imagine Dr Maudsley to be looking at the students.

Props and Furniture

All the students need to be seated, but that does not necessarily have to be on chairs. When they arrive, the women might take the last four seats, leaving the male students to perch embarrassingly on desks. This is the first time we see Miss Bott's knitting and reference is explicitly made to it, so here is the best chance to establish what she is making.

Costume

There might be a contrast between the more colourful and varied attire of the women, and the plain, dark colours of all the male characters' academic dress. The style of Miss Bott's costume might help to show that she is from an older generation than the students.

Lighting

If a director chooses to seat Lloyd, Holmes and Edwards among the audience, a low level of light on the audience seating may be needed for Health and Safety and to enable the audience to see the men when they speak. The more gradually this state can be introduced, the less jarring it will be for the audience.

Sound

The scene might open with a recorded effect of the hubbub of hundreds of students talking, to reinforce the impression of it being a crowded room.

ACT TWO, SCENE ELEVEN: VOTING DAY
Direction

As the play nears its conclusion, this scene is intended to present the audience with something new and unexpected. Introducing striking visual elements, such as the banners, and the energy of the riot, commands the audience's attention. As many actors as possible should be on stage during the riot to give the impression of threat and chaos; however, it is obviously important that the fighting is precisely choreographed and rehearsed with a stage-combat specialist. Moreover, the scene has the potential to be deeply rooted in theatrical tradition. Through its use of scapegoat (the effigy of a woman in blue stockings) and the idea of ritual celebration (the women preparing for their triumph) and destruction (by the rioters), the scene might be thought to reflect the origins of drama, which grew out of the Dionysian rituals of Ancient Greek society.

Set

The scene is set inside Girton College, which has been decorated with two banners proclaiming 'Degrees for Women' and 'Gowns for Girtonites'. Instead of the scene starting with a set-change in a blackout, directors and designers might consider incorporating the improvisation outlined in 'Practical Scene Synopsis' into the onstage action. The Girton staff and students can arrange furniture, climb ladders to hang banners or bunting, and share their nerves and excitement. There is something poignant about watching actors very carefully putting up decorations for their special day and then seeing it all torn down.

Props and Furniture

During the scene Will describes an effigy of a woman wearing blue stockings that the rioters have strung up and set on fire. The image is shocking enough, but might be even stronger if the rioters storm in pushing the bicycle with the smouldering effigy strapped to it. During the riot, furniture can be overturned and props destroyed. The mindless vandalism of a male student ripping up the women's books or tearing down the banners will create an impression of disorder and destruction for when Mrs Welsh returns.

Costume

The women might have dressed, optimistically, for a celebration, perhaps by putting flowers in their hair or wearing sashes like those worn by suffragists. They might even be proudly wearing blue stockings, in defiance of those who use the term derogatorily, and as a reflection of Jessica's own intention to reclaim the term. As with the set dressing, the process of the women adding these elements to their costumes could be part of the pre-scene action to avoid any delay between scenes.

Lighting

The ability of lighting to subtly affect the mood of a scene, to raise tension and to focus the audience's attention on a certain part of the stage, might be particularly helpful in this scene, where there will be a lot of bodies and a lot going on. For example, a lighting designer might use subtle differences in intensity to focus attention on the fight between Lloyd and Will, complementing the stage positioning to then immediately shift focus to wherever Mr Banks is punched.

Sound

Sound effects can be used to increase the tension as the rioters approach the college. The sound of an angry rabble jeering and chanting might get louder and louder before we hear the effect of windows smashing or doors being banged open offstage. The effects should be loud enough to startle the women, and if they come from multiple directions it would add to the sense of entrapment.

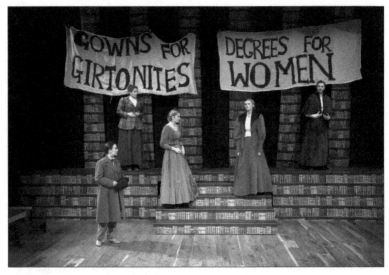

'Voting Day', photograph by Gary Wolff for Big Image Photography, in a production directed and designed by Ben Tait for Lady Eleanor Holles School, London.

Ben Tait's Reflections on the Design

My first thought for the design was that we needed the show to feel immediate and intimate: we wanted the audience to be inches away from the characters, and to feel part of the public scenes, such as the lecture. The bookshelves wrapped right around the auditorium, stretching high into the rig and sweeping in over the audience, to enhance the sense of enclosure in a rarefied world. I also wanted pace in the transitions so that the piece could match the vitality of the young women, hence the simplicity of the retractable steps and four wide, corner exits: basic period furniture could set each location swiftly and with minimal fuss.

Blue Stockings
In Production

Bristol Old Vic Theatre School's production of *Blue Stockings* (Tobacco Factory Theatres, June 2014). Directed by Donnacadh O'Briain. Photo by Graham Burke.

Production History

Jessica started writing *Blue Stockings* in 2008 and the play received its first public performance in October 2012. It was performed at the Royal Academy of Dramatic Art in London, one of the oldest drama schools in the country. Each year, RADA stages a number of full-scale productions that are directed and designed by industry professionals. Actors who are in their third and final year of training at RADA perform in the plays, which serve as a vital showcase, as well as giving valuable production experience, while the technical theatre students take on the backstage and design duties.

Jessica directed the cast of seven women and six men herself. The production was designed by Philip Engleheart and the music was composed by Laura Forrest-Hay. It was performed in the Jerwood Vanbrugh Theatre, which is a modern and flexible theatre based on a seventeenth-century design. It seats almost two hundred people, in a stalls pit and two balcony levels that curve around the stalls seating. The stage was configured in a standard proscenium set-up, which meant that the audience were sat in front of the stage and looked straight on to the action, which took place within the four-sided frame created by the proscenium arch and stage floor.

While the play was in rehearsal at RADA, Jessica was in talks with Shakespeare's Globe on London's Bankside about the potential of staging the play there. Although the theatre has a strong reputation for staging classic plays by Shakespeare and his contemporaries, it also stages new writing. In 2010, Jessica directed *Bedlam* by Nell Leyshon at the Globe – the first play written by a woman to have ever been performed there.

The Globe is a reconstruction of the late-sixteenth-century theatre that played host to many of Shakespeare's plays. Demolished in 1644, the Globe was rebuilt in the 1990s.

Although no one could be certain exactly what the original theatre was like, the location, design, materials and construction methods were all chosen to reflect the original design as closely as possible. The stage is set within an open-air yard, where some hundreds of 'groundlings' stand to watch the action. Other audience members pay more to sit on wooden benches in galleries that circle the stage on three tiers under a thatched roof.

Blue Stockings had its professional premiere at Shakespeare's Globe in August 2013, ten months after the RADA production. This time there was a cast of eight women and eleven men, plus two musicians. The production was directed by John Dove and designed by Michael Taylor, with William Lyons composing the music.

During the period between the RADA and Globe productions, Jessica made some significant changes to the script of *Blue Stockings*. The text of the play as it was performed at the Globe has since been published by Nick Hern Books as the definitive version, which has been performed by a wide range of companies in the UK and overseas. *Blue Stockings* has been produced by drama schools, university groups, youth theatres and amateur-dramatic companies, as well as being selected as a performance text for the Edexcel GCSE syllabus.

Rehearsal Diary

The following extracts are taken from the diary Jessica kept during rehearsals for the play at RADA.

Week 1, Day 1

Rather an odd experience, when words that have only been in my own head – and never heard aloud – suddenly get brought to life by the actors who will play those parts. When characters for the first time have voices and bodies. That now, when I write new lines, I can visualise who will be saying them. Quite a thrill.

The actors are really game, which is a relief. We kicked off with the readthrough, which always seems both massively disappointing, in the lines that actors don't quite land yet (it's day one!), and exhilarating, when you realise that they're already bringing new ideas to lines that I'd only imagined played in one specific way. Directing a play that I've also written is probably going to be double the work, but it's an opportunity like no other to shape the play as we go. I really want to have the script one hundred per cent fixed by the end of week two (of four), to make sure we have plenty of time to work on the performance, without the actors worrying about my changing lines late in the day.

Week 1, Day 3

I'm pleased with the new café scene (Mr Banks and Miss Blake) and the scene in the haberdashery, which was desperately needed. I can't quite believe it wasn't in the last draft. It wasn't until I went to Cambridge for research that I realised just what a big part class must play in this whole debate. If Lloyd has been brought up in elite circles and gone to Eton and then Trinity, it's no wonder he objects to working-class girls with no education turning up and seeming to put themselves on a par with him. And if he has had pressure from his father and family to do well and is already feeling the strain, you can imagine how the arrival of women, who seem to undermine the whole institution, could have a massive effect on his self-esteem. He's just trying to protect himself, to make himself feel better, but it comes out as rage. I really enjoyed writing that scene. It's good to hear where Lloyd's fear comes from. It now feels like the explosion of the second act.

Week 1, Day 4

Not keen at all on 'The Happiness Equation' [Act One, Scene Three]. It doesn't seem to be lively enough for that point in the girls' relationships with each other. It has to show them moving forward after their first lesson with Banks. We might improvise a more dynamic debate, just to see how that sounds. I read them some extracts today from *An American in Victorian Cambridge.*[18] There are accounts of students reading out their own essays in front of the class, so that might be one way of doing it. I don't think it's dramatic enough, but perhaps we could drop in on that or use that later. It's important that the audience realise just how clever the girls are, in order to feel the injustice of the fact that they were kept from their full educations. If we believe they have the potential to change history, to invent something that changes lives, to cure a disease, their being cut off in their prime becomes a tragedy rather than just a shame. That's what we need to aim for. The stakes need to be as high as possible, because they were.

I'm also not sure how clear the information about the vote is. The problem is it's just not interesting to listen to, and sounds like exposition. There must be a more active way of getting information across. Perhaps Miss Welsh could have a meeting with the powers-that-be? Or we can just slip it in in another scene. A scene with a bunch of tutors talking about the way the vote works would be deadly. No thanks.

Week 1, Day 5

I'm going to need to make edits to make a casting work. I don't want Ralph to be in the 'Wandering Womb' scene [Act One, Scene Four] but we haven't got enough boys to fill the hall so we might need him. Maybe I can keep him in the dark in the audience! I think that if we put all of the boys in the auditorium mingled with the audience for that scene, then keep the girls isolated on stage, it will help make it clear that Maudsley's audience is hundreds of men and just the five women. It needs to be terribly exposing when one of them speaks out. We might have to wait until tech to find out whether that works, but my gut instinct is that that's the best way to do it.

Week 2, Day 1

What a lot of rewriting I have to do! I'm trying to work out how best to use our rehearsals when I have such a lot of writing to do. Maybe just drink a lot of coffee and stay up all night? The actors have been inventing their own character histories, which they presented today. They were fascinating and full of details that I never imagined. Of course, I have my own histories for each of them, some details of which I've shared, other bits I keep to myself, but what's in my head and what they invent don't need to be the same thing, as long as what they're playing comes from a truthful place and aligns with the text. It is one of the joys of acting that there's a certain amount that they invent for themselves, which is the private inner life of the character.

Week 2, Day 2

Finally finished the script at 3 a.m., thank God! Will do all I can not to change it now, for the actors' sakes. Trying to write and direct at the same time is pretty crazy – I'm glad I'm not directing the Globe production. Think it's rather too much. Today, as well as rehearsing scenes, we're going to feed back from the two separate parties from the field trip to Cambridge. Half the students went to Girton, the others to King's, so we'll get a report from each. Then after lunch, I've tasked the actors with preparing a debate in character. The motions are 'Power is Knowledge' versus 'Power is Class'. Then I have an extract of *A Room of One's Own* to read them before we finish tonight.[19] My favourite quote, which inspired the play, is: 'Lock up your libraries if you like; but there is no gate, no lock, no bolt that you can set upon the freedom of my mind.'[20] A packed day on no sleep!

Week 2, Day 4

I have no words. That's the last time I leave a bunch of boys to do their own improvisation! I tasked the boys with improvising their college initiation. Let's just say there were naked wheelbarrows, snorting sugar, eating teabags, sliding across the floor, blindfolded races, singing, drinking – you name it and they did it. That scene won't be going in the play, that's for sure!

Week 3, Day 1

Today we improvised the boys making the effigy. Quite interesting to see how a practical task puts group dynamics immediately into the spotlight – who's the band leader, who's really got their heart in it, and who's got doubts? Lloyd, of course, was the ringleader. Holmes went along for the ride, plus felt it was important to do what their tutors had suggested and make their position known. Edwards didn't want to take part but was manhandled into it by the others being bullish; although when Lloyd thought it was funny to give the mannequin rather explicit boobs, Edwards backed off, not wanting to be insulting. It soon escalated into an argument where Lloyd told Edwards that he always flaked out whenever things got heated, and that this was their one chance to make a stand. Whilst I'm not sure whether we need this scene, it's certainly going to help when we return to the scripted scenes, in terms of how the group operates.

Week 3, Day 5

I have the flu. So does everyone else. It's not easy fulfilling writing and directing responsibilities simultaneously at the best of times, but getting ill this week has made me realise I'm not indestructible after all. The cast all have it. We're a bit at half-mast, but we're persevering.

The trickiest thing about this process is being responsible for the script and the actors at the same time. I've been making cuts this week. I didn't think I would but when you work through the scenes, challenges crop up, moments you want to add, clashes, repeats, length – all things which a quick edit could solve. But I really do want to let the actors run with it now, and stop fiddling. As much as the play might be minutely better if I keep on making changes, it won't be good at all if the actors don't know what they're doing. So I'm going to have to grin and bear it.

I've also found this week that, more than in any other process, it's been helpful to do improvisations around the scene to put relationships (more than events) in context. That work supports the development of the actors' characters so much. For example, we improvised Maeve and Billy at home when she tells him she wants to leave to study. We also staged the family dinner where Tess tells her folks that she's got in to Cambridge, then ran the improvisations straight into the scene which related to them, and it was transformative! I'm not sure whether this is specifically because it's a new play, but it's been the most helpful work we've done in rehearsals

– better than Actioning the text or any of the research. Just allowing the actors to know who they are and play in character in scenes that inform their scenes in the play… magical. Of course, it helps enormously that they're a supremely talented bunch.

Week 4, Day 1

I want us to spend more time with Ralph and Tess but there's no room in the play. It's going to be too long! So I'm thinking about writing some vignettes that we could play over the scene changes – them meeting to go to a concert together, them kissing in the orchard, them having a snowball fight. I think it'll help to show the passage of time and to make it clear to the audience that theirs is a real relationship, that they spend time together and that they are both investing in a future together.

Directing Perspectives

JESSICA SWALE

The experience of directing a play that you have written yourself can be very revealing and is not something that many playwrights get the chance to do. Here, Jessica reflects on her process of writing the play, how she approached directing it at RADA, and what she learned from the production at Shakespeare's Globe.

When you first started writing the play, what sort of theatre space did you envisage it being staged in?

I expected the play to be performed in a relatively traditional indoor space because I tend to imagine plays in the theatres from the era in which the play is set – rather than the era when they were written. I have seen the play performed in a studio, which was great, but in my head I imagine it in a Victorian-style space with a proscenium arch. There's something about that architecture that reflects the right moment in time. Something a little formal, which can be broken down by these women who want to burst out of their conventions and into the wider world. At RADA we played in the Jerwood Theatre, a conventional proscenium stage. Even though that is a relatively modern theatre, it has all the elements of a traditional turn-of-the-century Victorian theatre, similar to a lot of theatres in the West End and around the country. But we sometimes placed actors in the audience to break out of the mould. In the Maudsley lecture scene, he spoke to the audience as though they were the hundreds of men assembled, and we put the boys in the audience so that their responses came out of the dark. The girls, in contrast, had to sit on stage, near Maudsley, which picked them out and made it far more intimidating for them and, of course, more embarrassing when Tess speaks out.

How did that thinking change when you knew it would be staged at Shakespeare's Globe?

It was really interesting to rethink the play for the Globe. It had never been my intention that it would play there. It was a complete delight when they announced that they wanted to do it, so I rewrote a lot of scenes in order to make them physically work in that space. I reset some scenes outside. For example, scenes that had been in Tess's bedroom, I reset in the orchard. I think it's fascinating that a necessity often leads to more creative decisions in the process of dramatisation. I love the fact that Tess now has many of her emotional moments in the orchard. I like that we associate Tess with nature and know she likes to be outside, where she feels grounded. People often feel that they can speak their minds more easily in the open air. It's important that she is out in nature, under the stars, where she feels comfortable and where she can study the sky – her greatest passion. 'At least in an orchard I know where I am,' she says (p. 85). That discovery would not have happened had I not been forced to reconsider the location of those scenes, to avoid having to bring bedroom furniture on and off!

What did you envisage the audience's role in the play to be?

The use of the audience varies so much, depending on the performance space. At RADA, for example, we set the Maudsley lecture with all the boys sat in the audience and suddenly they were part of the two hundred people in the room. We couldn't do that at the Globe because at the Globe you can see the audience – there's no 'lights down' in open-air theatre. Yet, at other points, the audience seemed more alive at the Globe. Mrs Welsh addressed the entire space when she read out Tess's essay, for example. Everyone fell silent as she spoke to them directly. She could make eye contact with them, and managed to bring them into the scene as if they were the Senate. That sort of interaction can be magical.

Is it important that the audience feel implicated in what happens onstage?

I think so. I think that performing the opening intercut lines other than directly to the audience would be very odd. I wanted the audience to be addressed and therefore implicated. I like the fact that the women in the audience feel excluded from the first few lines of the play. Maudsley addresses the audience as 'Gentlemen', and immediately half the audience is isolated.

I have heard people mention the idea of dividing the *Blue Stockings* audience by gender, and having two banks of seating, one for men and one for women. We are not used to being segregated and, whilst it could be divisive (and annoy anyone who'd come to the play on a date!), it would be interesting to see if it worked. It reflects the time of the play to set up the idea that men and women were seen as completely separate beings. There are many psychological studies that show that dividing people into groups makes people feel those separating elements of their identity (gender in this case) much more viscerally. It would be interesting to experiment with that.

In the version of the script that was performed at RADA you wrote that, if roles need to be doubled, actors should ideally play characters with contrasting political views. Do you still think that is important?

I think it is interesting for audiences to see actors playing contrasting parts, partly for the joy of watching an actor transform, and partly for the interest of the juxtaposition of views. It's also important for simply being able to follow the story. There are a lot of characters, and if an actor plays two similar parts, it may be slightly more complicated for the audience to work out that they are not the same person.

I think it is also interesting to see an actor playing polar opposite parts in terms of the characters' politics, because it sheds light on the diaspora of opinion, but I don't think it's vital. It's more important that it is clear to the audience. We are currently looking at touring the original Globe production and, if we do, we will have to halve the number of actors, and everybody will have to double. Edwards might even have to be played by a woman, which would be interesting and throw a lot of things into the air.

Can you imagine the play being performed with an all-male or all-female cast?

I suspect that would be really hard. I think it is better that the men play men and the women play women, but there might be a few exceptions to that. You could have a comedy Miss Bott that was played by a man, or you could have Edwards played by a woman. However, I endeavour always to write interesting roles for women, as there are far fewer interesting parts in the canon for women. It's vital to hear women's voices on stage, so I would think that to stage an all-male version of *Blue Stockings* would go against the principles of the play. Also, the play is *about* gender, so I think it's great to show that in the most real light one can. But I'd never say never.

What did you learn about the play when you were directing it at RADA?

I learned a great deal about the play in rehearsals at RADA. One of the greatest opportunities that that process afforded me was to have time to explore which story to tell, and to work out who we were interested in. Before RADA, the characters had only existed in my head. Then, suddenly, there were actors attached to each character, and they all needed complete character arcs. Having a group of actors that I felt responsible for forced me to look at every character's individual story and ensure that each had a complete throughline and interesting pay-off. I never want to have a bored actor in a play that I have written. Perhaps because I was a director before I was a writer, I feel it's my responsibility to make sure an actor is happy in the rehearsal room!

One of the biggest bonuses of directing the play myself was that I could have conversations with the actors. One of them might say, 'I don't know what happens to my character. He just fades out' and then I could go and write them an ending. And certainly, when something wasn't clear to an actor – when they couldn't work out why they behave the way they do, for example – it gave me reason to look again at what I'd written and, if necessary, to clarify it.

The other benefit of that process was that I had a chance to hear the text, and therefore to work out what was missing. For example, I wrote the haberdashery scene during the rehearsal process. When we started rehearsals at RADA, I knew I wanted to understand why the boys felt so angry that the girls were at Cambridge, but I hadn't known how or where. Then, when we read the play, it was obvious where the scene needed to go and that it should be Lloyd who would say it. That scene is now one of my favourite scenes in the play, because that argument gets put centre stage and we see Lloyd at his most emotionally charged. It is a scene that often gets performed for auditions, as it's so dramatic, but there was a time when it didn't exist at all!

What new things did you appreciate when John Dove was directing the play?

I loved working with John. He is so clever and so generous, and was kind in giving me plenty of time to talk through the play with him in advance of rehearsals. That meant that when rehearsals began I didn't need to be there all the time, which is, frankly, of great benefit to everybody! I adore being in rehearsals, but I do think actors feel like they need to please the writer, so often it is helpful to give them a bit of space to make their own discoveries.

The process also taught me that a writer can never be possessive of their work. We have to hand it over. In writing a play, we do the first stage of the creative process and it's important to respect and give space to the bit that happens next, where other people are allowed to add their elements in order to build the production. For example, John would sometimes direct a scene in a way that I did not expect. At first that made me nervous, as I always had a set idea of what I thought a scene ought to look like, but, inevitably, by the time I saw it two weeks later when he had finished working on it, it would be not only different to what I'd imagined, but better! John has a different sensibility to me, and bringing together the perspectives of a thirty-year-old woman and an older man, with different life experiences and interests – those simple differences between us meant that we had different tastes and ways of looking at things, and when a scene had both of our influences, it would be better than my singular version.

Were any scenes in the Globe production different to how you had envisaged or directed them?

I had always imagined the boys' drinking scene to be rowdy and raucous because it was inspired by my experience of male students playing drinking games at university. In my imagination they were rowdy boys getting drunk together, but John had them all dressed in white tie and carrying genteel candlesticks, with classical music playing at the top of the scene. It suddenly felt like it was set after a formal meal at college. At first, I thought it ought to be fun and drunken, with the boys jumping on the table. As we see them in a formal setting at other moments in the play, I thought this scene was their one chance to contrast with that and to misbehave, but John said that they could retain that energy within the structure of the scene. Of course, by the time they had spent a few weeks rehearsing it, the scene had all the energy I expected. Yet rather than being rowdy in a modern way, there was form and dignity to it, which reinforced the idea that Trinity is a hallowed institution. It somehow seemed crueller, then, when Ralph celebrates his new conquest. What's more, when Edwards stood on the table to sing it was really an electric moment. That surprised me. It was brilliant, but I did not know it would work until I saw it.

Which scenes are the hardest for directors to bring to life onstage?

I think the riot scene [Act Two, Scene Twelve] is the hardest, simply because of the numbers involved. If it was a film, the girls would go to the riot in Cambridge. I wanted that to happen in the play, but it was not physically possible given the number of actors that we had. At the Globe we talked about putting the riot among the audience, to create the feeling that there were thousands of people on the streets, but it was just too risky and would have meant asking the audience to participate, which is very tricky. We therefore kept the scene set at Girton. I always wish that there are more people to be involved in it. It is great when the play is performed with a big cast because there can be a lot of people on stage, which is the way it would have been in reality. There were hundreds of people who came back to Cambridge to vote against the girls' right to graduate. It's lovely to get some sense of that bulk of people, and the threat they present, in the room.

Whilst the riot scene is tricky from a logistics point of view, I think the teaching scenes are the hardest tonally. It is vital that Miss Blake's scenes are exciting, sparky and quick. She plays an intellectual game with the women, testing, challenging and tricking them. When it is played too slowly or formally it loses that energy. The audience do not necessarily need to follow every element of the argument, but they need to get the feeling that the girls are taking off and rocketing into an intellectual sphere beyond what is expected of them. It is the same in the viva scene [Act Two, Scene Ten]. When the girls talk about the temperature of a star or the movement of icebergs they need to be alive with the excitement of this knowledge. It shouldn't be stultifying. As an audience, we won't necessarily understand the science or have the background, but we need to see that *they* do, and that they are fired up to speak about it. That should be enough. These are not girls who need to stop and think for a long time. They know this stuff and it is popping out of their mouths.

What is the lasting impression that you want audience members to take away from having seen the play?

I think it's important that an audience has a moment to take in the facts on the banners at the end: that it took fifty years after the riot before women were allowed the right to gradu-ate from Cambridge. It's a fact I still find shocking, and that's why I think it needs to be presented visually, to leave the audience with a lasting impression.

I have seen several productions where an actor has spoken the words at the end, but I would urge people not to do that. I purposefully chose not to set that section as spoken text because it's too important to miss, and it ought to stay in the room, quite literally. One production I have seen used a voice-over, and half the audience heard it, but half the audi-ence didn't. I feel strongly that directors and designers ought to do whatever they can to put the text up. If I had wanted Tess to say it, I would have given the lines to her.

In terms of the wider impression, I write to give people an emotional experience. I think the play has an important mes-sage about the value of education and the rights of women, but I also want it to be a good story, which sweeps you up and imaginatively engages you. As Mark Kermode says in his film-review programme, a good film should make you 'laugh at the funny bits and cry at the sad bits'. I have tried to write a play that does both; if I can do that, I'm happy.

JOHN DOVE

Prior to directing *Blue Stockings*, director John Dove's work for Shakespeare's Globe included *Anne Boleyn* and *In Extremis* (now renamed *Eternal Love*) by Howard Brenton, and Shakespeare's *All's Well That Ends Well*, *The Winter's Tale* and *Measure for Measure*. Here, he reflects on his approach to this play and considers the historical under-standing that fed into his work.

Did you work with Jessica in revising the text for the Globe production?

Yes, all the way through, and it worked very fruitfully. I loved working with her because she was so open and things could keep bubbling up. It started with getting a heroine – a main runner – and then working the play around that. If you've got a heroine, you can take the audience off on a narrative journey and they gradually become less aware of the respon-sibility they hold until a moment like the end. Jess is an absolute blueprint for how to be imaginatively open and then morph it into an incredible structure. The Brontës and Shakespeare opened up, and Jess has this ability to be open and at the same time is a tremendous artist who paints her own canvas. Unlike Dr Maudsley, she isn't afraid of ideas, but sees them as a platform to dive off.

As a director, what initially interested you about Blue Stockings?

We are storytellers – I am not talking about gender, but about stories. Nearly fifty per cent of the stories of humanity have not been told, and it is our responsibility to get them out. Gender comes into it because a lot of what women encounter is because of difference and prejudice, but as a result of that the narratives have not been told. It is no good telling a story simply because it is about Elizabeth I; you want to tell a story about a seamstress the night before

Queen Victoria's coronation. Start to pick out the stories that you would naturally tell if they were about men. Arthur Miller was always interested in the janitor, and was never interested in the king; with that came the janitor's wife, and not the queen. Certainly, in *Blue Stockings*, that was where Jessica was coming from, as with [her subsequent play for the Globe] *Nell Gwynn*, and it is a wonderfully healing way to approach narrative.

Did that make Blue Stockings *particularly suited to being staged at a theatre like the Globe?*

The Globe is a public forum, which is why the doctors of the church kept trying to close it down in Shakespeare's time. I have done plays by Howard Brenton and Helen Edmundson there and they all have the same growth point: being present in front of a lit audience. You are not quite debating with the audience, but you are very much in the public domain. It is about opening a door and saying, 'Follow us and we will tell you a story.' The essence of the Globe's storytelling is that it brings the audience to a point of wanting to debate, but the narrative part is always slightly stronger, so they should not debate until they have gone.

How might that sense of inclusiveness be achieved in a different type of theatre?

When we take the play out on tour we will be behind a proscenium the whole time, but we will begin with players going out into the audience and talking to them before the opening scene. Then in the interval the musicians will be on stage and the actors will come out again. That is to try and create the same feeling – it doesn't necessarily need to feel boxed in.

How did your direction respond to the unique demands of Shakespeare's Globe?

We were going to use a form of fluid movement anyway, and literally create different pictures on the move, whether we were indoors or outdoors; so be it the Globe or wherever, that would have been the way to do it. One or two scenes are only a few lines long, so you want to keep it rolling, and we didn't have any trouble doing that. We had a lot of continual music underneath, blending the narrative so that anything that needed to be brought on, such as the library, was brought on very simply. That is exactly how I would do it again.

What effect should the play have on the audience?

Alfred Hitchcock said that an audience will not emote if they are thinking, so do not let them think. I say that about everything in the theatre. Instead, let them get involved and then quietly point out what they are involved in nearer the end. The punchline comes right at the end of the play on the banner, so we tried to involve the audience in the narrative rather than sitting them down and accusing them. I do not believe in that. It is very important to give as even a floor as possible by turning it into a debate and giving everyone their side, because at the end the play comes up with the fact that there were no degrees for women until 1948. The words came down on banners and when they began to come down, people thought it was going to be a celebration; it was not until they read what was on them that they realised.

What were your priorities in rehearsals?

Trying to do two things: the first was trying to make the actors feel at home in their environment and the character they are building, and the other was keeping an eye all the time on the narrative. So Tess comes in thinking one thing, then somebody says something and she thinks another thing; then somebody else says something, and she questions the first thing and whether she should go back to it.

What was your understanding of the journey that Tess goes on over the course of the play?

Tess is facing two incredible challenges: falling in love and trying to come to terms with science. To me, the heart of the play is that if you let the muse land on you, how much do you give up of your personal life? Tess has found out she has got a big brain, and then she falls in love. She knows, given the world as it is, that if she follows the love through, she will be sacrificing a huge passport to freedom. The more we could fill out the tremendous journey that Tess is going on, including finding a boy, the more it ignited her mind in every way.

How important was the issue of gender to your approach to the play?

I think that, because they are all challenging themselves mentally so much every day, to some degree the gender issue is moved to one side. If Tess is sitting there trying to work out a theorem or equation, she does not sit there thinking, 'I am a woman trying to work out an equation': it is her mind that is trying to do it. She would be sitting there reading Darwin and not thinking of Maudsley – she would be thinking of Darwin because that cannot do anything but fill her mind. At the time, the women were being blocked from all around because of their gender, but within the cauldron in which they were working, their preoccupation was with how to think in a way that would match, and exceed, the academic fire that was burning in the colleges. If their teachers were prepared to take them on their mental strength, they could get to a point of being listened to, regardless of gender. That, in a way, is liberty.

I am so thankful that the play really is about that, and is not about a gender battle. The gender battle is the starting block, but the race is ten minds at work. When the play thrived there was a feeling of ten people running a 100-metre race, with the stopwatches held by minds – not by men and women. It is the same as during the Olympics. Athletes are not at all interested in the time differentials between men and women, because that is a given. What is interesting to them is how the women have prepared and how the men have prepared, or who has got into a zone and who has not. When there is a phenomenal female gymnast or diver, the others all want to know what kind of energy quality they are summoning from the zone, not what time they do. That is irrespective of gender, because it is to do with inspiration.

The great thing that was done with discussion and rehearsal was shifting their awareness away from 'Oh my goodness, I'm a woman' to 'How do I solve that?' I was after that baton-change from awareness of gender to being hooked by the muse. In a way, that rendered the young women vulnerable; they were no longer on their guard in the gender battle because their minds were not thinking about it. Then they would be brought up short because somebody in a tea shop would say, 'Oh, you are a woman.'

How did you help the actors to understand their characters?

It was about saying at the beginning of each character's voyage – including their voyage in each scene – that the circumstances they were in meant they had no idea what was going to happen next. That is because there was no map for what they were doing. What did they do if they were thrown out? What did they do if they wanted kids? What did they do if they could not get the work right? There was no map for anything, other than this enormous testament in brick or stone to bright minds that, in the past, were men. They had to ignore that, or flip over into an almost ungendered state, for example by looking at Einstein for his science rather than the fact he was a man. Otherwise, they would have been finished.

How did you communicate the sense of the students' tremendous intellect through the performances?

We tried as much as possible in the viva scene to make the to-ing and fro-ing unfollowable for an audience, who might then be sat there thinking, 'We don't know what they're talking about any more.' To create that world we tried never to slow down. If the audience saw Tess talking with a tutor, they might not follow any of it. In that case, the moment she fails hits home because we know it is not because of her intellect, but because she did not do her revision.

How might the reactions of Professor Collins and Professor Radleigh influence the audience's understanding of that scene?

There is no question of gender in those interviews; they are not judging them as women. They are talking to people who might become scientists. Women had never been viewed in that way before. It is like the female athletes of today who are judged as athletes, not as women, and they move into a differ-ent zone because the context of the competition is not gender. Collins and Radleigh are after scientists, so that scene is about potential, regardless of gender. If they thought Tess was not capable of doing the work, they would somehow have told Mrs Welsh. The first thing Mrs Welsh would have said to them would have been, 'Do you think that under other circum-stances she has got it?' They would have said, 'Yes, she has got it.' That is why Tess is allowed to stay. Those two tutors are interested in Tess, Carolyn and Celia; you cannot play that they are trying to knock them down because they are women.

Does that make it worse for Tess when she fails?

The humiliation for Tess of not having done the homework is enormous, because they were saying, 'We are not judging you as a woman. Have you done the work?' Tess knows bloody well that if she had been fit, she would have got through. The battle is within her. There is an external battle with people like Maudsley, but to some degree that takes second place to the battle in her mind, as she knows she has not done enough because of her choices.

How important is an understanding of the historical context that the characters are living in?

You cannot overestimate the influence of Queen Victoria in this time. She was an astonishing trailblazer. Telling Albert he had to wait to marry her was revolutionary, but we never see her like that: we see her as a young woman with a crown on her head. She had exactly the same problems as Tess. She had something that she believed in and that was a massive responsibility, and then she fell in love. Nobody gave her much of a chance at the beginning, but she surmounted all that and was the most powerful woman in the world. Then she collapsed, because her husband died. A lot of people were saying, 'We can't give women these pole positions.' It was a big subject in Victorian society. She went into mourning for forty years and we are now discovering that she actually did undertake a lot of engagements, but to the outside world she was the woman in black. That was alarming, and a lot of the men seeing Girton starting out would have been saying, 'We've been through all this and it doesn't work.'

Scenic and Costume Design

A WORLD OF BOOKS AT RADA

At RADA, designer Philip Engleheart's set was a world of learning and of books. Six towering flats designed to look like wooden bookcases were positioned on tracks that allowed them to move laterally across the upstage, mid-stage and downstage. Some of the bookcases had doors or windows built into them, while another held actual books that were then taken off the shelves during the library scene. In between the bookcases, trucks that had furniture positioned on them added a slightly raised playing space. To make full use of the theatre's fly tower, additional set pieces, such as a bedroom fireplace, planks of wood representing trees in an orchard, or bunting and banners, were flown into place. The floor was painted in a colourful, geometric pattern to look like oversized Victorian tiles.

In the void space around the bookcases, Philip made use of another potent symbol of learning: handwriting. A set of handwritten rules for students were painted in white (to look like chalk) on the black rear wall and floor space around the tiles. Furthest upstage a staircase curved up offstage and a heavy oak door standing in isolation allowed for entrances to Girton College. Above those, white panels were built into the architecture of the building and lit like a cyclorama to suggest day or night when scenes took place outside. In front of the lit panels, a row of books in silhouette was suggestive of a town skyline in the distance.

Here, Philip describes the evolution of this design, from his initial research trip with Jessica to Girton College to the opening night.

How did you find inspiration for your design?

Research is something I really love doing to understand the world of the play I am going to create. I did a lot of research through books, but we also set up a trip to Girton College. I had found a lot of interesting stuff about education, women, bicycles, architecture, costumes and the politics of the period, but the Girton archives were fantastic for giving us actual pictures of people we could identify as the characters. We sat and picked the girls out of the year group photographs!

How did you then apply the research you had done to the text itself?

I drew a storyboard of the script, so that I could see the scenes, with a code to say how many pages they were. If an audience is looking at something for seventeen pages' worth of action, they need seventeen pages' worth of stuff to look at. If the audience are looking at something very slight for a long time, it sometimes feels like they deserve a bit more. I do not really design from the long scenes outwards, but I certainly pay attention to the long scenes and make sure that those can be served, and then I look at how the shorter scenes are being served between them. The other thing I do is look at where the emotional pictures are. When I draw storyboards, I draw the emotional moments that happen in each place. Most scenes have at least one emotional moment – that is why they are a scene – and if a scene does not, that usually means it is about information or transition.

What sort of emotional moments did you identify?

There are certain key moments, like Gertie [the character that evolved into that of Tess – see Character Profiles chapter] trying to get out of the window to climb down into the orchard. However that is achieved onstage it is an act of rebellion and of going against the laws of the college, it shows her personality and character, and we see her friends react to her trying to climb out. The window is therefore an emotional point, so it is really important that all the audience can see it. There is no point designing it on stage left where half the audience can see it and the other half pretend to see it. It was not quite centre-stage, but it was as good as.

What practical considerations did your design have to take into account?

One of the obvious things was that there were at least twenty different locations, if not more. Some of the scenes are very quick and some of the scenes are sat in for twelve pages. It was very clear that we could not afford scene-changing time for a scene to last just half a page, so we looked at how it could be slick and quick. From a designer and director's point of view, the question is how absolute, architectural and real you make the settings. The more you make it absolutely real, the more there is to move off, change or transform for it to become the next space. So we already knew that it would be a more stylised set.

What were your initial ideas for the scenic world of the play?

We knew that the play was about learning, and that it was Victorian. Perhaps the fact it was about Girton was a slight red herring. There are scenes outside Girton, so it cannot be set *in* Girton – because how would those scenes work? I held off making it architectural from the word go, because I was much more interested in seeing what else it might be first.

I was interested in what the experience was about. We looked at a lot of students' writing. There were letters home and people writing their exams and lessons, so handwritten words seemed very important. There was one point when I thought the set might just be walls with handwriting all over them. There was one letter home that had a drawing by the student on it showing the room, the shelves and where she put her flowers. We were going to do all the sets drawn in pen and ink but we decided that, because there were so many of them, it would end up being very busy, and might have become boring.

I knew that there had to be some sort of Victorian holding shape. One of the very early ideas was that Victorian iron-work could define the space, but that did not quite feel right. I looked at the research of all the rooms and all the interior spaces we had seen, such as the Senate House in Cambridge, and started designing spaces inspired by a corridor, with dark-oak walls at the bottom and pale upper levels. The idea was that the upper level could represent the sky and being outside, and then inside it would feel much more contained. We worked with that idea, but again the issue was how big objects like tables and chairs would come on.

In terms of furniture and set dressing, how did you and Jessica determine what each scene required physically?

Jessica is really good at keeping action on its feet, so we were looking at using the minimum furniture. In every library there is a table, because that is where you sit and do your work. It would be very hard to do an examination in an exam-ination room without tables. We were asking what would undermine an actor in doing each action if the physical object was not there. So it was decided that Gertie would need something to climb out of, even if it was a block or a table on its side that represented her leaving the window. However, there is something about opening a window, or a window being closed and then open, which is physically more inter-esting than miming a window; I wanted there to be physically something that was opened, so that we understood what 'closed' was.

The same logic must apply to doors, which you used in your design even though there were not really walls for them to sit in.

It is really interesting seeing somebody who is going to answer a door getting ready to answer the door. That is a very good clowning exercise. If I am the head of Girton answering the door, what do I do beforehand to present myself? The audience can see that, because the wall is see-through, so there is comedy, drama, pathos and tension in it. Having two sides of a door where you can see people arriving from both can become really interesting.

After all those initial ideas, how did you decide on using book-cases and handwriting?

I kept on looking at the pictures and it was funny that it had not leapt out at us first, but in all the rooms, behind all the furniture, there were just walls and walls of books. It was obvious. That was the turning point. I just realised the walls should be walls of books, the doors and window would be in the walls of books, and the walls of books would fade into the heights so that you could not see them finish. The whole point of the play is that they are there to study and, at that time, studying was about books.

One of the other things that we had held on to was a picture I found with the rules for the students written out in hand-writing. That ended up being copied word for word onto the set in white writing on black, like chalk on a blackboard. The rules and the play are all about whether they can leave and go out on their own, so the idea of having those rules on the set became really important.

How did other aspects of the staging complement the set?

We storyboarded all the transitions and then Laura [Forrest-Hay] took them away so that she could see what the movements were going to be, and compose music for the sequences. For example, when the set moved into the bed-room, the fireplace came in, the window and door moved in and the trucks came in with her furniture, as the other trucks from the previous scene went off. The absolute treat is when, on the last beat of the music, all of them have arrived and they all stop at the same time. In the same way as the music was very balletic, so were all the transitions. That is the ballet of theatre and it really underscores and supports the poetry of Jessica's writing.

How did you use props, like the bicycles, to enhance our understanding of the world the characters live in?

I wanted the boys to turn up en masse on bikes the first time we saw them, to give the idea that the boys were very mobile, but the idea of woman on a bicycle was a thing to behold, to be laughed at and for effigies to made of. That is another different emotional dynamic that I wanted Jessica to be able to make on stage. We spent hours trying to convert the stalls and engineer a ramp so that it was possible for lads on bikes to ride through the audience onto stage level. If they come on from the wings, it is not as exciting as coming through the audience. I was adamant that the boys had their bikes in rehearsal for longer so that they could ride them really fast on stage.

Was it important that props and furniture were from the correct period?

I am keen that if the audience are seeing so few props, they see props that are authentic to that period. I was really holding out for bikes that were properly of the period. It is the same with any other prop in the piece. If there had been a 1950s armchair instead of an 1890s chair that would have really mattered to me. Object research can be very interesting. Try to find handwriting of the period and how printed things, like campaign flyers, from the period were typeset. I researched knitting patterns from 1897 to see what Miss Bott would be knitting and what the knitting needles would have been like. One of the hardest things as a designer is that there is no limit to research.

Case Study: Opening the Play

The play started with a downstage black curtain lifted just to knee-height so that all the audience could see were passengers' feet, wheels, suitcases and steam. It did not show the whole of Cambridge Station, but just where the action was. Philip kept thinking about what he would do if he were designing for a film, where the camera would have been at knee-height, just showing the hems of the dresses. Since the play was written in a very filmic way, he and Jessica decided to do exactly that on stage.

Once the stage had cleared and the curtain was raised, Dr Maudsley was seen standing stage right and Mrs Welsh was stood stage left. Above the upstage-left door was a banner reading 'Welcome to Girton'. Maudsley was lit in a harsh, white light through a gobo screen in the outline of a window, while there was a much softer, warmer wash on Mrs Welsh's side of the stage. The different lighting states instantly communicated the idea that they were in two totally separate locations, and emphasised the theme of a gender divide.

Both of these visual themes were returned to later in the play. The lighting state used for Maudsley was used again when Mrs Welsh addressed the Senate in Act One, Scene Thirteen. Likewise, the end of the play returned to the same visual shape as the opening: as the downstage black curtain slowly came down, projected writing appeared line by line in a typeface that echoed the handwriting all over the set.

The female students were dressed in vibrant and distinct colours – green for Gertie, a deep rust for Carolyn, grey for Maeve and camel for Celia. Why did you choose those costumes?

I always use colour very carefully in costume. I think it helps an audience to navigate their way through a cast when there are a lot of people in the same group, such as groups of girls or lads at college. We could have put all the girls in black skirts and white blouses, but I did not want to do that because I think their world is much more interesting. When the women are put in dark skirts and white blouses it takes away some of the joy in their lives and the fact that clothes were one of the few choices they did have; they did not have a uniform to subvert, so they could make their own call. I also wanted a contrast against the boys, who were in subfusc. In this story the audience need to hold on to the women most, so I was very keen that each of the girls was endowed with a colour.

Green was a really nice character for Gertie because it is symbolic of a young, fresh, growing thing, like a new shoot. We chose a pale-green suit for Ralph too, so that made them match as partners. Carolyn was always going to be in gorgeous rusts. I wanted her hair to be pre-Raphaelite red, so she was always going to be dressed in dark green or red to go with that. We researched the Arts and Crafts movement and what was to go on to become art nouveau and art deco. She is the window into that world and is forward-looking, so her clothes were all a bit ahead of the period. The foreign influence was built in because of the French influences in art nouveau. Carolyn was also moving into more of the kimono or *happi*-coat look, whereas the other three girls were still in the cut of the period: tight bodices, puffed sleeves and fairly tight skirts. Carolyn's costumes were much softer around the neck and bodice and she was the only woman on stage not to wear a corset.

We wanted Maeve to be in a very drab, 'servant' grey as though her patron had said, 'Can you make her a sensible school-uniform suit?' Maeve had probably been given the choice of any colour but had gone, 'I'll just have charcoal grey please,' because her personality would not let her go beyond charcoal grey. We chose a really rough wool that would be itchy – like a hair vest – as though she was saying, 'Don't notice me and don't spend any more money on me, I will just have that cheap wool.'

How did you costume the scene where we see the Girton students in their bloomers?

I knew that later in history the women would have pulled the backs of their skirts through their legs and tucked them into their waistbands, so I was keen for that. But the whole joke was about the bloomers themselves, which Jess was really keen on. We talked about whether the women should have taken their skirts off so that they were just wearing their bodices and bloomers, but I felt that they would *not* have done that. That would have been outrageous! So we got them to tuck their skirts into their bloomers. That was a slight 'director–designer off', but would a woman really have taken her skirt off? I was sure that she would have done everything she could to keep the garment on and still get on the bike. That is why we had that ridiculous scene where their bloomers were filled with their skirts – but it fed the comedy of the scene and I think it worked.

How can costumes help to differentiate between the ages of characters?

I tend to choose darker colours for older people. The younger teachers were in paler suits, but then the older the dons got, the darker their costumes were, until they ended up being in black. Mrs Welsh was in high-status, high-age dark colours and the neckline of her dress was high, like a choker. Hair and make-up also help the audience when actors play different characters. We decided that all the boys were clean-shaven and all the male adult teachers had moustaches, although it is really hard to play all the way through with a moustache stuck on! We also discovered that Trinity gowns were blue, whereas all the other colleges had black gowns, so we brought in blue gowns for the boys from Trinity.

The set of the Shakespeare's Globe production designed by Michael Taylor and directed by John Dove.
Photo by Michael Taylor.

ARCHITECTURE AT THE GLOBE

At Shakespeare's Globe, designer Michael Taylor's set was imagined as a blueprint that was just beginning to take form. The set consisted of two large printed cloths in wooden frames, with two slender pillars downstage of them, and a walkway stretching out into the yard where the groundlings stood. The colour scheme was very simple: dark-blue pillars, dark-blue fabric wrapping the Globe's two large structural pillars downstage, and white for the backcloths. The cloths showed architectural drawings from the period in which the play is set, and on each cloth the drawing was becoming three-dimensional as though it was an idea becoming realised. Modern light bulbs hung over the set and were inset into the frames around the backcloths, and at the end of the play two scarlet banners unfolded from the roof.

Here, Michael, who has worked with John Dove many times over the past twenty years, explains how they formulated a design that worked with the unique architecture of the Globe.

What was your initial thinking behind the set design?

The origins of the set were a combination of different factors. It's a modern play and we wanted the set to feel modern, rather than just a representation of Girton College. Consequently we were looking for a visual idea to take us away from naturalistic reality. The story of the play is the realisation of a new idea: women's education. Girton was a new college for women, so we aimed to present that in physical form, with the architect's drawings becoming real in front of us.

How did you decide on the design that was printed on the backcloths?

We looked at photographs of Girton, but for the set we used architectural drawings by the same architect, Alfred Waterhouse, for a different building – Manchester Town Hall, in fact. I think this was just because they looked right, and we could get high-resolution photographs of them from the Victoria and Albert Museum. The fact it wasn't Girton wasn't important. We were doing a play, not a documentary.

Originally we were going to combine the architecture with other images, in particular a drawing called *Angel of the Revelation* by William Blake that also expressed the invention of a new ideal.[21] We were also going to have images of study overlaid on the drawings, and perhaps biological and botanical drawings, but in the end we decided all of that would be distracting. In fact, I recently found an earlier version of the backcloths, with a more complex image on it, and I wondered whether we should have gone with that rather than the simpler one we ended up with.

What practical considerations did you face designing for the Globe?

In 2013, when the play was produced, there was very limited lighting at the Globe, and what was there tended to be a bit murky and unable to pick out the actors from the background, as normal stage lighting needs to do. So, in all the productions John Dove and I have done at the Globe, we have tended to use very pale or white backgrounds, so that the actors register most dynamically. The permanent architecture of the building is a riot of colour, so part of the purpose of the design is to still it and simplify it. Dark blue is a good, still colour and echoes the blue on the ceiling of the 'heavens' [the raised roof-structure supported by the pillars on the Globe's stage].

How did the architecture of the Globe inform your design choices?

Another of the Globe's problems is that the big pillars are surprisingly far downstage (in the opinions of some, they are too far downstage even for historical accuracy). The effect of them is that, if an actor stands in the middle of the stage, which should be a strong position, a proportion of the audience can't see them. So John Dove always brings the action right downstage to get away from the pillars and improve sightlines. That would tend to leave all the actors in a line along the front, so we always now use a walkway into the yard so that the action can come into the audience and actors have a reason to be downstage and facing the audience. In fact, two or three metres out on the walkway is the strongest position for an actor at the Globe, as it's nearer the middle of the circle of the building.

Another consequence of bringing all the action right downstage is that it tends to leave the upstage empty, so we always try to think of something to fill the space. In this case it was two pillars. Their only purpose was to fill the upstage area so that it didn't look as though someone should go there! We had to make entrances in the bottom corner of both backcloths, which meant fairly careful positioning of the image on the cloth so that it wasn't too disrupted. The Globe stage also has a central entrance and we put a curtain over this that could be drawn back by a stage manager behind, to provide a silent quick entrance.

How did you decide to dress the students and what informed that decision?

We wanted to stress the seriousness of the students and their struggle, rather than going for something much prettier which the 1896 date would have justified. It was a period of elegant dresses with masses of fabric and lace, and we wanted to avoid that and keep to something more dramatic and modern. So all the young girls were in skirts and blouses with jackets, and nearly all the men were in suits.

Which pieces of stage furniture and props did you decide were essential?

We kept all the furniture minimal. We put a shelf around each of the big pillars, which was useful for props during the play, and under them, on each side, we had three or four bentwood chairs, which are light and of the period; some were stained dark and some were stripped wood, as though they – like the architecture – were in the process of being made. We had a table on wheels for the scene in the haberdasher's shop, and a smaller dressing table on wheels for the bedroom dressing table, both of which were painted off-white. For the scene in the library we needed a library table; it was very long but only thirty centimetres wide, so it could be brought on and removed very quickly. This sort of cheating is totally possible at the Globe in the interests of telling a story. At the Globe, although the architecture is a challenge, it also enables you to simplify; because there was no lighting and hardly any set, an actor can walk on with a lantern and say, 'Here we are in the orchard at night' – and we are there.

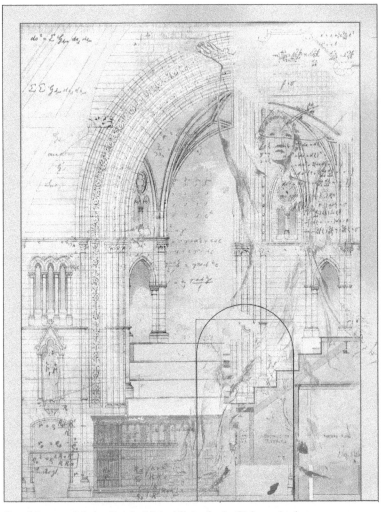

One of the unused design ideas by Michael Taylor for the Globe production.

Music

RECORDED SOUND AT RADA

Composer Laura Forrest-Hay had worked with Jessica on a number of productions, including *The Belle's Stratagem* (by Hannah Cowley) and Sheridan's *The Rivals*, before collaborating on the RADA production of *Blue Stockings*. As a trained actress, Laura's work on a production is also guided by collaboration in rehearsal, and she and Jessica used music to enhance the cast's understanding of character and the world of the play. Her original score was based around two musical themes (one masculine and one feminine), plus a romantic refrain, and has since been made available for licensing to use alongside the play.

Here, Laura explains how she discovered the world of the play musically, and responded to the demands of the production.

What was the focus of your initial conversations about music with Jessica?

I had been to quite a few of the readthroughs so I was feeling familiar with the world of the play, and we knew that we wanted the music to do quite a few different things. Music can help set the play in a particular period, but one of the main uses of music was to create a female world and a male world. We could help that element of the play musically, so I made certain decisions with that in mind.

How did your impressions of the distinct male and female spheres inform your compositions?

Obviously the whole score had to marry as a piece, but we decided quite early on that we wanted the music around the boys' scenes not to have so much tune or emotion but to be driving forward. The male characters have that sense of ambition and entitlement, so that was a world I wanted to create around them. The boys' theme was called 'Entitlement' and it was all about percussion; there was some piano in there, but it was very staccato and rhythmic. For the female characters, I was much more struck by the idea of learning and self-advancement – that sense of stretching and pushing oneself and overcoming challenges. The girls' theme was called 'Learning' and there was another called 'Blue Ribbon', which was more about the romantic relationship. The two main themes for the women used much more lyrical piano and built on themselves by reaching further each time they repeated. It was a way of us showing the women constantly climbing and moving forward, but was also quite cyclical in the way that they were going round and round politically and not getting anywhere.

How did research inform your approach to the play?

One of the things I researched was the world of music at that time. What would the girls have listened to? What would they have had access to? How would they have listened to music? For example, I researched the Gramophone and we decided that, although they had been invented, they would not have been widely used domestically, so maybe the characters would have had music lessons or listened to concerts or gone to shows. Carolyn has got money and travelled, so we decided that it was possible she might have had access to a Gramophone; it would not have been common, but it was possibly something they could have got hold of.

I made a list of the hit music of the day and what was happening. For example, Carnegie Hall opened, so one of the characters might have been aware of that, and certain pieces were being written. Elgar's 'Enigma Variations' were being composed, and so were Mahler's First and Second symphonies.[22] I would listen to those things to get into the world. That is not to say that I necessarily wrote nineteenth-century pieces, but I wanted to know what was happening so that, even if I was not doing that, I knew exactly what I was going against.

I also find that research is helpful for actors, so I will share this information with them. Some of them might choose to listen to it to get into character and maybe we will listen to a bit in rehearsal. Music immediately brings you into a world without too much chatter. I find that research has many benefits; all that stuff is really helpful to me as a composer, but it is also something I can share with the cast as a very easy keyhole into that world.

Was there any research or preparation that you did that was not used, but could be helpful for people working on the play to know about?

Jessica had already found 'Gaudeamus Igitur', but on the route around that we found many more college songs, which I had thought we could use in rehearsal. We could have spent a session on a song and seen how it feels to sing it. I read that a lot of the students changed the words and made the songs quite rude. Could we do that in an improvisation? Would that give a sense of camaraderie or flouting authority that the girls had to have? We did not do an awful lot of that in the end, but I did share the work with the actors so that they were aware of the history of these songs. I found out that Mrs Welsh wrote a song called 'A White Sheet' when she was a student at Girton in 1872–3. Stuff like that can be really lovely to use in a rehearsal or for the actors to be aware of. Even if it does not come into a three-hour session, it is always there on the wall or for me to talk to an actor about.

'A White Sheet'

In the early 1870s, three of Girton's students became the first to take the Tripos exams. The women became known as 'the Pioneers' and college songs were written in their honour, including one by Elizabeth Welsh who was a student at Girton at the time. 'A White Sheet' is a parody that contrasts the women's work and love of learning with Cambridge's complaining male students and their terrifying dons. Each stanza ends with a celebration of the fact that being in Hitchin means the Girton students are free as birds to leave 'Old Cambridge' behind.

How do you shift from doing all that research and immersing yourself in the musical world of the play to composing your own music?

Before we start rehearsals, I go away and write a piece of music that reflects the way I feel about the play or characters in it. That piece is not supposed to sit anywhere in the play, but is just me expressing my reaction to the words and what I have seen in the readthrough. When I have that overall theme, I know that the rest of the score will be taken from it. If I really crack into that essence of the emotion of the play and its core feeling, I can use it afterwards, pull it apart and repeat bits. It helps me creatively because it provides me with material, but it also helps the play because most of the score is coming from that one potent place. Even though the audience will never hear the whole thing in its entirety, I feel that it has a genuine, honest connection to the play. It really worked for this play because I had a very strong feeling for it, and responded to the girls stretching themselves and their expansion, resilience and constant ambition.

What techniques or instruments did you use to create a sense of the Victorian period?

The piano was the obvious one and was really appropriate because it can be very fluid and lyrical, but also dramatic, strong and rhythmic. It has got so much variety. It was also the correct instrument for the era, because piano was the modern music of the time. Debussy's 'Prélude à l'après-midi d'un faune' came out in the 1890s, so they were moving into a time of beautiful, impressionistic piano. I felt that there was something very beautiful, lyrical and feminine about it. Somehow it has the ability to be happy and sad at the same time, which I was drawn to for this play because there is so much to celebrate, but at the same time it is devastating at the end when they do not get their degrees. I also used clarinets, which set it in a certain period because in the romantic era the clarinet was used a lot.

Other than that, I was using quite modern percussion and drones. I had a very high drone and a very low drone going. The audience would not necessarily notice, but drones help a lot. There is a change in the tension in the air and you might not be able to pinpoint what it is but you can just feel it. My own influences are things like Steve Reich and mini-malism, so that had to come in somehow.[23]

The only time I wondered about live music in the produc-tion was whether there might be a piano on stage for someone to play; I figured that, in the evenings, they might have done that.

Did you write anything that was entirely Victorian in style?

In the RADA production, Ralph sang the poem that he reads to her in the orchard. That was probably the most period piece in the whole score. Although it was original, it did sound as though it could have come from that era and I ended up using it to bookend some of the scenes that he was in. Because the world of the play is Victorian, the emotional language is slightly repressed. I think that there is a good argument for the music to be a bit more emotional than the characters are. That was the order of their day, but I felt much more freedom because I was not writing Victorian music. I was writing modern music with the sensibility and instrumentation looking back to that world, and that allowed me to be much more emotional in the music.

How was your work informed by being in the rehearsal room?

Although I will write the one big response before the show starts, once I am in rehearsal I react to what happens on the floor – how scenes are ending, what we need to bring up next, what are we looking forward to, and what we are going to introduce next. I think the rhythmic stuff possibly came out of some improvisations we did with the cast. We were doing exercises exploring the rhythm of different types of walks and entrance. What is the sound of that kind of entrance when six boys come barrelling into a lecture room, full of beans? What is the energy of that? We used rhythm a lot for the boys and when they were improvising we would have stuff going on behind them, to give the scene that sense of drive.

It sounds like your work in the rehearsal room helps the actors to explore their characters as much as it helps you when composing. Is that an important dialogue to have?

Music should not be just an add-on at the end; it should feed in right through the process from before the first day of rehearsals. I think that is really important, and Jess and I work really well together because she thinks so as well. I was an actress myself, so I see music as a key to open up characters. How might a rhythm affect an actor's movement or open up a line reading? Music should be a tool for the actors as well. In my workshops, if actors are not playing instruments, they are doing some sort of rhythm or voice work to make music that might open up their characters or a scene.

Can warm-up songs be an easy way for directors to incorporate music into rehearsals?

Absolutely. Doing the school song is a very quick 'in' at the start of a session. When I worked with Katie Mitchell, we were creating this slightly fascist world for a Greek play [*Iphigenia at Aulis* at the Abbey Theatre]. I wrote a national anthem for the cast to sing. I do not think it made it into the production, but we did the national anthem of this fictitious country every day as a warm-up. That sort of thing is where music can pull a group together really effectively, and bring anyone who has had a bad morning smack-bang into the world before moving on to the text.

How did the music respond to the episodic structure of the play?

One of the challenges of the play is that there are a lot of scene changes, and as a composer you have to be very careful that you do not extend those breaks, while still covering whatever needs to be done. The music becomes some sort of link that keeps it all moving and keeps the momentum during those short scenes and the scene changes. Taking the music from one big piece is very helpful for this type of play, because then the ear is not dipping in and out of brand-new stuff, but is just returning to things that keep moving and ploughing forward – just like the girls did. When you've got short scenes, you cannot keep jolting people out of the action; you've got to keep them going right the way through, so that they don't feel like they have watched twenty-five scenes. Music is really important and can make or break that: if you keep putting in new bits, that is just going to distract.

What are your tips for people working on the play who may not have lots of resources?

I would steer clear of using different pieces of music for each scene change. Try to find two or three pieces that are going to serve your purpose and that you can edit if necessary, and don't overload the play with lots of new music that pulls people's ears away from the text. Be true to what the characters are doing in the story. Although I provided cues for pretty much every scene change, don't be afraid of not having a cue if you can get away with it. If the set and costume changes allow, just barrel on through, because it's better to have nothing than to crowbar something inappropriate or too long in. Don't use music for the sake of it; the play doesn't need it – the scenes move very well on their own.

How did music fit with the other design elements of the production at RADA?

I was so taken with that set: watching those beautiful book-cases was like watching a ballet. Knowing what the set is doing is very important to me when writing music, and in that case it was beautiful to score what Philip [Engleheart] was doing. Although I said you've got to keep everything moving on, sometimes when you have short scenes happen-ing very fast, you need to let the audience absorb it for a second as well. You don't want them feeling like they are being beaten round the head with fast-moving action for the entire first half, so there's nothing wrong sometimes with allowing a moment of contemplation. The set was moving so beautifully that there were moments in the score where it was doing the same thing and being reflective, to allow people to catch their breath before the next bit.

Did you use music to underscore the action and create emotional responses in the audience, or was it mainly about linking scenes?

I mostly stayed away from the text. At the beginning and end of scenes music would creep in and out, so that it was a bit more seamless. The only bits that were deliberately under-scored were the romance scene in the orchard and when Gertie gets thrown out of the lecture. There is an awful moment just before Maudsley throws her out, where he tells her to pack up and then goes into that horrible speech about women. That *was* underscored, but it was the very low rhyth-mic stuff to pull us through. You want to create a feeling, but not be in someone's head. I wasn't describing what she or Maudsley were thinking at that point, but I wanted to highlight the tension that was there. It's not about creating emotion, but it *is* about atmosphere and taking the tension up a notch to let the audience know it's building into something else.

How did you stage the closing song 'Gaudeamus Igitur'?

First, we had to make sure that the actors all knew what it meant, so I gave them the translation and the background to the song, and we used it in rehearsal to get their voices warmed up.

I really wanted to create the sense at the end of the play that it was a movement that continued, even though we see them failing to get their degrees. We did something quite adventurous, so that there was a sense of one voice becoming many voices. We recorded the girls singing the song, and the boys singing it as well, and then we layered it up, so that from four voices there became sixteen. We kept layering it up and up so that it sounded like there was a distant crowd singing it. We kept the men's voices separate and only brought them in towards the end, because they only came on board as the rest of the world came on board.

I arranged it so that it started with a live voice on stage. The actress had to have an earpiece so that she could get her note and come in on time with the backing track, then the other girls joined in, one by one, so that there was a four-part harmony happening on stage. Gradually the track crept over the speakers from front-of-house right through to the back of the auditorium, so that by the end the effect was of an enormous crowd singing the song.

I was really passionate about making that work, and the sound crew at RADA were very patient and enthusiastic about trying to create that effect. There were clever things they could do so that it didn't sound like one voice layered up a hundred times. They slightly staggered the tracks, so that it had the effect of a massive choir. That had much more impact than just the four girls singing it, and by the end we had the whole cast on stage, plus the backing choir coming through the speakers.

I felt very emotional when that went along with the projected words saying that the women got there in the end. The emotional heart of that production was what those women started, and how we benefit from what they did. I was constantly shocked by the final projection. Every time the words came down, I could not believe that I didn't know about that, at my age and as a feminist. I think there is still a rallying cry to be heard and there is an ongoing battle that is not over yet. For me, and I think for Jess, it was very important that we were throwing something out to the public, who could then carry it forward.

LIVE MUSIC AT THE GLOBE

The music for the Globe production was composed by William Lyons, who has had a long association with Shakespeare's Globe and has worked with John Dove on a number of productions there, and on tour. At the time of *Blue Stockings*, the Globe used only live music and not amplified or recorded sound, although that was to change a few years later under the subsequent Artistic Director, Emma Rice. William composed for a three-piece band – a percussionist who also played piano, a trombonist, and a trumpeter who doubled on a flugelhorn – who played from a balcony at the rear of the stage. The other significant change was that the play ended with an original song composed for the production rather than 'Gaudeamus Igitur'. John Dove says that decision was taken 'to create a counterpoint' to the content of the banners, 'rather than underlining it'.

Here, William explains the unique challenges of composing for a theatre like the Globe, and the thematic vein his music captured.

How do you and John Dove work together when composing music for a new play?

John is very thorough. Unlike other directors, he will have a meeting with me before starting rehearsals. We will go through the entire text and he will have a very heavily anno-tated script. Sometimes we will not have the finished draft, which is how it was with *Blue Stockings* because it was a work in progress. With every show he works on, he has thematic devices – he talks about a love theme, a tension theme, or a thriller theme. Those adjectives are not necessarily to be taken at face value, but are indicators for me of what combi-nation of ideas I can work with at a particular time. If you have a theme for a particular person, or a mood for a partic-ular scene, threading its way through the narrative, they can come back as leitmotifs, even if just as a subtle reminder to the audience of where we are aurally.

What was the central recurring musical theme of the play?

I was coming up with ideas for what the opening scene with the bicycle could mean, and that gave me the theme that went through the whole play: motion and progress. For me, that scene is wonderful because it gives motion, joy and a rush of youth that represents the whole struggle that then ensues in the whole play. The style I wrote in for that scene was *música repetitiva*, like Steve Reich and people like that. The audience wouldn't notice it, but hidden within the music are cycles of harmonics and patterns in circles like the wheels of the bike. That theme kept coming back throughout the play, in differ-ent minor-key versions, different voicings and different instruments. That was the thematic motif, even though it was a rhythmic motif rather than a melodic one.

How important was the music of the period to you?

When I do the music for a historical-practices production I will more or less draw music from the period and arrange it to make it fit the drama, with very little actual composed music. With a play like this, the ostinato theme of movement, cycles and progression was very modern, but the cancan was in the style of the period. A couple of pieces I put in had a sort of tea-dance, Scott Joplin, ragtime-type feel to them.[24] That was all happening around the late-nineteenth and early-twentieth centuries, so it fitted in very well.

What inspired the song that the cast sang at the end?

Elgar was writing around this time; he was young, but he was known in that early period. There was a whole school of English composers – Butterworth, Vaughan Williams and Elgar – who were all coming out of this new emergent sense of an English idyll, along with Tolkien and C. S. Lewis.[25] I based the song – the anthem – on Elgar's 'Nimrod' Variation. It was my own piece but it referenced that and 'Jerusalem' as well. I wrote the lyrics, which were supposed to be idealistic and looking forward to the future, but nothing too specific. That then led into a company dance, in a style that was a bit like a ragtime cakewalk. The anthem worked very well as an end-piece that gave a sense of hope and unity. It started with the women singing on their own, and then everybody joined in, which is a good device because it is a nice way of symbolically uniting everybody.

What are your main considerations when composing music to play over transitions between scenes?

The trick is not to get too embedded in a compositional sense that creates too many melodies, although I am a great fan of writing melodies. With John, as with any director, I will write a piece of music that is not that long – perhaps a hundred and twenty bars – but it will end up being eight bars. I have become more economical about how I have written over the years because you know that things will compress, especially in a theatre like the Globe. John likes snappy scene changes that are very quick, so anything I have written will often get compressed.

How do those practical concerns influence the music you write?

You hear a lot of theatre music that is very simple in structure, because it has to convey things, concisely and precisely, in a short amount of time. You don't have a great developmental scheme, but have to say something very quickly. Sometimes that seems frustratingly perfunctory. A lot has to do with the style you write in or the way you set up a piece that you know could be of indeterminate length. If you've not got time to develop twenty-four bars into a melodic statement, you use a rhythmic statement. You have to have various ways of stripping down what you have got, while maintaining the intent and meaning by compressing all that into four or five seconds.

How do you work with musicians in that context? If you need to shave a few seconds off a transition, do you have to rejig the whole piece?

I will look at it and say, for example, 'Let's take out bars four and five and put bars six and seven in that place, but let's move bars eight to twelve to the beginning of the piece.' The band are very good and will come up with suggestions or help out in that sense. In tech, when I haven't got much time and there are lots of things going on, I'll do that very quickly, make a note of it and then go away and rewrite it to fit the time frame. Obviously, one show later it will go back to what it was in the first place. I always tell people never to throw anything away, but to put it to one side because they might come back to it. Usually there are one or two cues that come back to what you started with.

Would you use music to reflect on what has just happened in a scene, or to look forward to what is going to happen?

John is very keen that you do *not* lead the audience – you do *not* tell them what is about to happen before it has happened. You don't do 'Duh–duh–duh!' just before someone evil walks on and before they have done anything evil. I am reacting and colouring what is there, rather than announcing anything before it is due to happen. Another thing I do is born out of the Globe tradition of having an end-piece – a song or dance at the end of the show. That can be seen as a conceit, but they do it and always have done, and I have always tried to come up with that bit first of all. Then when I write, I am thematically referring to points the audience are going to get later in the play, even if it's just a few bars, or the harmony or the melody.

Did you use music to underscore scenes?

It's funny because, having given me the structure, John will find inspiration from the tech week and I will suddenly find a lot more space for music is allowed. A lot of directors and actors fear being undermined, rather than being underscored, and they worry that music will detract, so you have to balance it very carefully. Underscoring is very common in TV and film, but it's a dangerous device to use in theatre unless it's carefully set so that it doesn't lead people too much. If someone's delivering a speech, you don't want the audience to be pulled a certain way, in particular with a play like *Blue Stockings*, which is intensely intellectually conceived. You are not using music to beat people round the head, so you've got to be very careful when putting music into a play like *Blue Stockings*, which is far too delicate to start being too obvious with music.

Was there a scene where underscoring did help?

We had to set up the scene in the library fairly quickly. There's a great deal of humour in it, but there's also a certain amount of tension, and we did use underscoring there. The piano played a very light, repetitive motif that carried on and built up. At the end of the scene that would sit under there, but brass would take the mood into the next scene. Layers are how you bind it all together: you keep one idea going, and then layer up on top of that to lead you into the next scene.

What particular considerations do you have when composing for the Globe?

When I've worked there we haven't had any recourse to electrical, acoustical enhancement or subduing of the sound, so you have to be very careful with where you place music so that it doesn't intrude or dominate. Acoustically, the Globe is brilliantly designed. Unless there is pouring rain, or people are talking, you can make it work with the right combination of players and instruments. You often end up having more music in a play at the Globe than you would in other productions. You fulfil all those other things that sound designers and lighting designers can do, because you colour whole scenes with just a bit of music.

You can also use space, although for *Blue Stockings*, other than for a bit of pre-show music on stage, the band were in the balcony [the musicians' gallery overlooking the stage]. For other plays at the Globe, the band might play outside in the piazza, in the upper galleries where the audience are, or up in the stairwell to create distance. There are actual spatial effects you can achieve by physically moving the band. There are lots of plays where that really works, especially a Shakespearean martial play where you can have trumpets and drums playing from different places in a battle scene. However, Michael Taylor's design for *Blue Stockings* didn't allow for any movement outside of that central gallery because we had artificial wings put in, which actually helped to boost the sound by acting as amplification boards. Also, there just didn't seem to be any point. There was talk of having the band come marching on when the banners go up, but then they would have had to get back to play the song a few lines later…

How did you decide which instruments to use?

It was very brass-oriented. The practical reason for that is that you can hear brass instruments better than you can string instruments, and there are quite a few occasions when there are big events in the play or songs that the actors have to be able to hear. Also, I like the music of the period and a lot of it used brass instruments. You can do a lot with brass instruments – you can mute them, you can have various sound effects with them, and they can be quite lyrical, as well as full-on. Given that it was just a three-piece band, they did a remarkable job.

How should people with limited resources approach using music in the play?

If you don't have a lot of resources – for example, if you only have one person playing the piano – be mindful of how that person is going to enhance the drama. That could be a few notes or chords between scenes, or it could be something more substantial. Also, find out what the actors can bring to it – and if there are any good actor-musicians in the company, make use of them. Do your homework: even if you don't use music of the period, know where it is coming from. The advice I would give to anybody writing music for a show is: never think it is all about you. Never think you are writing a great magnum opus, because you're not – you're writing music for a play, and you are not the most important thing. Funnily enough, when that happens, you will probably write much better music.

Character Study

In the RADA production, Verity Kirk played the central protagonist, Gertie Moffat, later renamed Tess. Verity was in her final year of training, and *Blue Stockings* marked her first industry performance at RADA, which she had joined at the age of eighteen.

What did you identify most with about Gertie?

I identified with her most at the beginning of the play, in the sense of really desperately wanting an education. I could compare that with how much I wanted to go to drama school to train. There was also that exciting feeling that for the first time in your life you are being stretched, pushed and tested, so I identified with that. I found it slightly harder to identify with letting a boy overcome that, because I have always been good at not letting boyfriends interfere with my acting! At the same time, it was interesting to think of her as a late-Victorian girl and realising that this is the first time in her life that all these experiences have happened to her.

How did you balance her being a trailblazer with the sense that she is a product of the Victorian period?

My natural instinct was to play her very strong, with a kind of twenty-first-century female view that girls going to uni for the first time is amazing! In a really good way, Jessica said to tone it down, because they were not like that and there would still have been that degree of respect. For a long time, Jo in *Little Women* [by Louisa May Alcott] was my go-to reference.[26] When Jessica said that was too strong, I started thinking about Marianne Dashwood in Jane Austen's *Sense and Sensibility*. That was the best reference I had, because she is very smart but also very romantic, and Willoughby takes her off on a journey she should not go on.

I used to listen to a lot of music from the *Sense and Sensibility* film soundtrack, even though it is from a different time period. There is a scene where Marianne is walking in the fields and she looks at Willoughby's house after he has got married. I used to listen to that bit of music on repeat before I had to go on and find out that my character had been dumped by Ralph. It would always get me to the place I needed to get to. That was a technique people used quite a lot at RADA, and although I had never found it particularly did anything for me, for this play I found it so evocative and I always used it. At some point it would probably have lost its charm if I had been doing it in a real run. I can't listen to that piece now because I just cry when I do!

What did you do to understand the world they live in?

I read the book *Bluestockings* by Jane Robinson, and I looked into what Gertie's daily routine would have been like. They would have got up very early, and it would have taken them a long time to get ready, do their hair and get into those dresses. She would probably have been reading while she was having her breakfast and would have been constantly taking notes and thinking. We did a lot of work on the academic subjects they would have studied, and I know someone who studied History at Cambridge who said the amount they were expected to read was just beyond comprehension. Girton was a long way away, too, so they would probably all have been walking to lectures together and testing each other on what they had been learning. When they got there, they would have been hustled through all the boys staring at them. They would always have been learning and never had any downtime. They probably didn't want time to rest, and if they ever did stop for a moment they probably got the other girls to come and test them. You could never let up, because you had more to prove than anybody else.

How does her relationship with the other Girton students evolve over the course of the play?

It is interesting to think that they are all new to one another's behaviour and to how they respond to different things. Celia doesn't understand Gertie's behaviour because Celia herself would never act like that. You judge other people by your own expectations, and at first they barely know one another. It's similar to being in a cast with someone, when you knit together very closely because you are doing a shared thing.

How significant are experiences like the Maudsley lecture in bringing them together?

That scene felt really humiliating and made us really angry – but then we couldn't show that anger because as girls we were trained not to. What is *really* annoying is that Maudsley is proved right: he can go home and say they aren't suitable. That is even more infuriating. She was absolutely right, but he is going to go home and think that he has been proven right. Sometimes the bad people win... although you're not taught that when you're little.

In the draft of the play that you performed, the character that evolved and eventually became Will was actually written as her brother, Charlie. How did you build their relationship?

I talked to Pete [Hannah, who played Charlie] about what our home life might have been like, how our childhoods may have played out, and what our parents were like. I remember us thinking that our mother was really beautiful, elegant and smart – someone like Cate Blanchett. There is that great story about Gertie climbing his classroom roof, but when they got a bit older Charlie would have been sent away to boarding school and she would have been lonely and consigned to doing all the girly things. He was probably the best brother, because when he got back from school for summer or Christmas he would have taught her all the things and given her his old textbooks so that she could be on the same level as him. I found knowing all that really emotionally strong for connecting in the scenes with him.

Did you feel it would have been hard for Gertie to persuade her family to let her go to Cambridge?

I always thought that it would have taken some persuading. Her parents were probably middle-class, gentrified, incredibly intelligent people themselves. She would have been surrounded by books her whole life and they would have encouraged her to find out as much as she was able to. There would have been a worry about what other people thought, but also a sense that they had encouraged her to pursue knowledge her whole life, so why would they stop her at this point? I remember reading that when the actress Emma Stone was a child she did a PowerPoint presentation for her parents saying all the reasons she should go to LA. I thought that Gertie probably did a seminar about all the reasons why she should go to Cambridge. She is such a strong person that they probably thought there was no stopping her, and no point making her miserable. Charlie would probably have played a huge part in that. He would have said that she deserves to go and that he would look out for her. The stakes are high for him because he has promised that to his parents, so both of them are going to be in trouble if she messes up by getting involved with a boy.

Why does the relationship with Ralph sweep her off her feet so quickly?

It is a first romance: the first time a boy has been interested in her, and interesting *to* her, in that way! She has probably thought all the boys she has met to be stupid and ridiculous, and they probably thought she was weird and reads too much. Ralph is fascinating to her. He is this beautiful creature and he has picked her out of all those girls. Also, it is secretive and all those things that appeal to teenagers. In a lot of ways her emotional development would have been behind ours, because of what she would have been kept from. When you are fourteen, fifteen or sixteen and you have your first boyfriend, it is all-consuming. She feels like nobody has felt like that before, nobody will feel like it again and nobody understands how huge those emotions are. Also, Tanmay [Dhanania, who played Ralph] was great because he is really easy to do scenes with, so we talked a lot about what he liked about her and what she liked about him. The idea that you don't have to be completely sexless, asexual or not appealing to men if you are a successful woman is really important from a feminist point of view.

How did you approach the scenes towards the end of the play where it all comes crashing down?

It was always horrible doing those scenes one after another because they were so sad. She gets dumped and then she fails. It is heartbreaking that she has thrown it all away and lost everything. The solidarity of support she receives from the other girls – that bit Celia says is very moving – and the generosity of Mrs Welsh were all moving to me as a person, so it easily fed in to her. She is probably going to be a stronger person for it, and is more emotionally mature because of it, so it needed to happen to her in order for her to go on and become the extraordinary person she is going to be. You can be as book-smart as you like, but if you don't have some emotional development, you are never going to get there.

What do you think Gertie went on to do when she left Girton?

When she went to Cambridge, she would have wanted to be a politician or somebody really high-flying and in the spotlight, but by the end of it I think she would have wanted to be a lecturer. I think that the inspiration of Elizabeth Welsh, and the kindness she shows Gertie, would have meant she would want to give something back. That was always the thing I felt really strongly about her. She would be somebody who would feel that she has a debt to pay back for girls like her.

What was the hardest thing to play about her?

I found it hard to play a heroine, because you have that responsibility of wanting people to like you. At RADA I had mainly played character roles, where your job is to be funny or supportive. It is not necessarily to be the person that the audience latches on to. I tried not to think about the responsibility of being the person on stage that the audience want to follow. Also, you hope you do it justice. After you have done all that research and thought about all those women and their supporters, you wonder what they would think if they came and watched. How wonderful it would be to have them there and to think that it does them justice.

How did Blue Stockings *prepare you for your work professionally as an actor?*

It was a really good experience of working on a text that was still developing and had a later life. It showed the gestation of a play – how long that could be, how much work went into it, and how many people were behind it. It gave me a chance to take a lot of the skills I had learned in the previous two years and implement them. Being in a new play that had a journey was interesting, as was being in a play that was saying everything I wanted to say. All the theatre I have done since I left RADA has been stuff that I feel is saying something important and speaking to people. *Blue Stockings* is the kind of play you want to be in and feels important. When I watched the film *Suffragette* I realised that I had a mine of knowledge from doing *Blue Stockings*. I always value that about any play: it gives you a pocket of knowledge about a certain era of history that can be so important. Sometimes you feel like you have degree-level knowledge in completely different things.

What tips do you have for people playing the role in the future?

Just enjoy her. Joy is the thing to embody about her, until everything comes crashing down. If you do really root for her, it becomes dramatically and theatrically interesting and impactful. She is before her time and has done things so that we don't have to struggle. Savour the character because she is an example we should all follow. Education is so precious, and it is terrifying to see how much people have to pay to go to uni, and how much pressure they are under. There is no sense of enjoying learning any more. That is what this play celebrates – the joy of being given a chance to learn. She does fail and lets herself down and that should be an example to us, too, because the education system puts too much pressure on us to always be good, and society puts too much pressure to always be perfect. It is important to be shown women who fail; there is no shame in failing, because that is how we learn.

INTERVIEW WITH ELLIE PIERCY

By the time the play was seen at Shakespeare's Globe, the central protagonist had been renamed Tess. The role was played by Ellie Piercy, who had considerable experience working at the Globe, including having previously worked with John Dove on *All's Well That Ends Well*.

What was your initial connection to Tess and what appealed to you about the play?

Tess is wonderful. She is instinctive, skilled, sensitive and throws herself into things, predominantly showing all her faults and how life is a challenge in many unpredictable ways. I loved that, and it felt easy to relate to. She was also a wonderful heroine to reveal a story through. The play is about the experiences of women trying to be true to themselves, fighting for their rights on a very basic level and working out how on earth to manage what they deserve in life: love, stimulation and experiences.

What research did you find helpful to understand the world they lived in?

It was hugely important to know what was going on at the time socially, educationally and politically, while also maintaining that a lot of their experiences, feelings and thoughts are timeless. I loved looking into other stories from the time of women who didn't do 'the norm'. The *Bluestockings* book [by Jane Robinson] was great for that. It's very easy to view the past, particularly the Victorians, as people with unimaginative ideas and boring stuffiness; but there was a lot of wildness and new things happening. Also, these are real people with hopes and dreams and energy – just different ones!

How did you approach building the character?

Each project demands a different approach. Too much research or history wasn't hugely helpful, moment to moment, for Tess, as the play seems to be about what keeps happening to her unexpectedly, and so she needed to be open and available to the 'new'. It's important to look through the script and find the clues about a character, and how they are perceived by others. That might be something to use or to work against. Also, rhythm in speech can speak volumes about a person's nature. Often Tess is quiet, and when she speaks up it seems it is from feeling compelled to speak truth. That, for me, made her strong and sure inside, but added an insecurity about her own view of herself and her inexperience. The play gives you the clues!

What decisions did you make about her home life, her family and their attitude to her going to Cambridge?

Only decisions that helped the playing of the scenes: for example, about how much her and Will had a sibling-like relationship, or how bored she was. In some ways, it seemed more appropriate that Tess had blocked stuff off while she was there, in order to cope, so my memory of things I thought were helpful at the beginning have faded. She needed to think that she didn't know what to expect at Cambridge.

How would you characterise Tess's relationships with the other Girton students and Mrs Welsh?

I think it was a delight and a challenge to form these relationships. I think Tess is a loner as well, so she doesn't need the girls, but is game for life and experiences. The others come into that and provide unexpected fun, love and depth of experience. Mrs Welsh is the mother figure – something that doesn't really come up elsewhere in the play, except in Tess's guilt. It seems as though Tess is much more her father's daughter. Mrs Welsh is a different female authority that nurtures and disciplines her. I love their relationship; it is not easy, but it is amazing, to have someone support you who is also stern and harsh at times.

What aspect of her character or story arc did you find hardest to understand or communicate?

We found the communal girls' scenes hard. We needed to create a world that didn't feel known, trite or insulting to their intelligence but that, at the same time, was fun, serious and unusual, because Girton was the first college of its kind. I personally found the astrophysics hard, and had to find a way to have a clear understanding in my own head to help me navigate through Tess's amazing academic brain.

Conclusion

The American writer Edmund Wilson once wrote that no two persons ever read the same book. And it's true. Every work of fiction will be interpreted differently by each of its readers. Think, then, how much more true that must be of a play, which is not only read by different people, but re-imagined with sound, voice and music, design and concept, reincarnated in infinite new imaginings by successive actors, and then interpreted by each member of its audience. That, as a writer, is a joy: to think that an idea that was once a private thought of mine, existing only in the personal space of my imagination, can now belong to, and be interpreted by, you and others who encounter it. It's a privilege, and it's exciting to me to see how others will go on to invent that world for themselves.

There is no one right way to stage *Blue Stockings*. I have seen many productions in a great variety of settings, each of which has found its own voice and brought the piece to life with a uniqueness of interpretation that is gratifying to watch. From studio settings to open air, school rooms to video-projection sets, the choice is yours. So if you are staging the play, enjoy the creative opportunities. Embrace the chance to delve into the characters. And follow your heart in your interpretation. This book should give you plenty of starting points.

We set out in this book to give you a contextual background to the play, to reveal the historical setting behind the action, and to shed light on its characters and drama. I do hope you have found it inspiring. Now it's over to you to bring the characters to life, whether you are directing a production, or sitting in an orchard somewhere, simply imagining Tess under the stars.

Enjoy it.

Jessica Swale

Acknowledgements

Thanks to all those who generously contributed their time and expertise in the writing of this book including John Dove, Michael Taylor, William Lyons, Philip Engleheart, Laura Forrest-Hay, Ellie Piercy, Verity Kirk and Sarah Kenny. Thank you to everyone involved in *Blue Stockings* at RADA and Shakespeare's Globe, including both casts and production teams and Dominic Dromgoole, Francine Watson Coleman and Katya Benjamin. We are also grateful to Gary Wolff and Ben Tait, Vince Haig and Eleven One Theatre, Jason Jamerson, Bristol Old Vic Theatre School and the Girton College archive for the use of images, and Matt Applewhite and all at Nick Hern Books for their guidance.

Jessica would like to thank Lois Jeary for her tremendous work both as an assistant director and as a researcher, and for her fantastic efforts in putting this book together.

Lois would like to thank the Jearys and her urban family for their support. She is truly grateful to Jess for being so open and trusting, and for inviting her along on this adventure.

This book is dedicated to the women who came before us and who paved the way for us and our daughters to live with the freedoms and opportunities that we enjoy.

Jessica Swale and Lois Jeary

Glossary of Historical Figures

The following is an alphabetical list of the historical figures and artistic works that are referenced throughout the play.

MATTHEW ARNOLD (1822–1888)

English poet and writer of social and literary criticism, whose essay 'The Study of Poetry' was first published in 1880. In it, Arnold makes the case for poetry having 'higher destinies' – the power to explain existence, and in doing so to complement and complete scientific discoveries, as argued by Carolyn in Miss Blake's moral science class (p. 54).

FRANCIS BACON (1561–1626)

English philosopher and scientist who advocated a scientific method based on observation of nature and inductive reasoning. The phrase 'knowledge is power' is attributed to Bacon, but misquoted by Celia in Miss Blake's class (p. 24).

LUDWIG VAN BEETHOVEN (*c.* 1770–1827)

German composer and pianist, whose career spanned the Classical and Romantic periods. In Mr Banks's class (p. 64), Holmes references Beethoven's observation that 'music is a higher revelation than all wisdom and philosophy'.[27]

BOADICEA (*d. c.* 61)

British queen who led an uprising against occupying Roman forces. Carolyn invokes her spirit when urging Tess to embrace the adventure of meeting Ralph (p. 48).

JAMES BRUDENELL, 7TH EARL OF CARDIGAN (1797–1868)

Brudenell is best known for leading the Charge of the Light Brigade in the Crimean War and lending his name to a popular form of knitted long-sleeve jacket, which Tess references when decrying women's invisibility in the major events of history (p. 84).

JEAN-MARTIN CHARCOT (1825–1893)

French neurologist who argued that hysteria was an inherited, neurological condition that could be identified in men as well as women. His work drew links between hypnosis and hysteria – a method that was criticised by some contemporaries. Tess refers to his work when refuting Dr Maudsley's position on hysteria in the lecture (p. 32).

JOHN CLARE (1793–1864)

As the son of a Northamptonshire agricultural worker, Clare wrote poetry that described rural life and nature during the upheaval of the Industrial Revolution. His poverty and background as a labourer chime with Maeve's own upbringing, so it is no wonder she quotes him in Miss Blake's class (p. 26).

NICOLAUS COPERNICUS (1473–1543)

Renaissance astronomer who, although not the first to do so, theorised that the earth revolves around the sun, which is at the centre of the solar system (a theory known as heliocentrism). His theory began a long line of discoveries and revisions from Kepler through Galileo to Newton... and then Tess. Maeve cites Copernicus as an example of a scientist who made a great discovery through the power of the imagination (p. 55).

OLIVER CROMWELL (1599–1658)

Initially elected as an MP, Cromwell rose through the ranks of the Roundheads during the English Civil War. Following the execution of Charles I, the Puritan Cromwell was made Lord Protector of the Commonwealth. He was educated at Sidney Sussex College in Cambridge and is one of the figures that Lloyd lists when telling Carolyn, 'We built this country. We made this nation' (p. 88).

GEORGES CUVIER (1769–1832)

French natural scientist, whose study of fossils (specifically, the negligible change between species over time) led him to critique Lamarck's theory of evolution. He also argued that, historically, species had become extinct after catastrophic events. During her viva, Tess fails to recall that in the early 1800s Cuvier collaborated with Alexandre Brongniart on a study of fossils in the different layers of sedimentary rock around Paris (p. 107).

CHARLES DARWIN (1809–1882)

Natural scientist who published his influential text on evolutionary biology *On the Origin of Species* in 1859, establishing the principle of natural selection. Darwin is mentioned as a contemporary of Dr Maudsley by Mr Banks (p. 30) and as a student of Christ's College, Cambridge, by Lloyd (p. 88).

DIOGENES (*c.* 412 BC–323 BC)

Ancient Greek philosopher who is considered one of the founders of Cynicism, which holds that the purpose of life is to live in accordance with nature, free from material desires or possessions. As Miss Blake tells her students, Diogenes' philosophical position was illustrated by the life he led on the streets of Athens, where he slept out in the marketplace (p. 25).

ALBERT EINSTEIN (1879–1955)

At the age of seventeen, German-born Einstein enrolled at Zurich's Federal Polytechnic School to study mathematics and physics. In the play, just the following year, Celia cites him as being 'quite ahead of his time' in her viva (p. 104). During his career, Einstein was responsible for hundreds of scientific papers and profoundly influential theories.

MILLICENT FAWCETT (1847–1929)

Fawcett was involved in politics and the suffrage movement from her late-teens onwards, and is considered pivotal in the campaign that resulted in women being given the right to vote. A moderate suffragist, Fawcett wrote, campaigned and built a reputation as a strong public speaker before presiding over the National Union of Women's Suffrage Societies for more than twenty years. She also co-founded Newnham College, where, in 1890, her daughter Philippa became the first woman to obtain the top score in the Mathematical Tripos.

GUY FAWKES (c. 1570–1606)

A member of the group of English Catholics who plotted in 1605 to assassinate the Protestant King James I by blowing up the House of Lords during the state opening of Parliament. The Gunpowder Plot, as it became known, failed, leading to Fawkes being convicted of treason and hung, drawn and quartered. Subsequently, it became popular to burn an effigy (known as a 'Guy') on Bonfire Night, which Will refers to as he describes the rioters' effigy of the woman wearing blue stockings (p. 111).

SIGMUND FREUD (1856–1939)

Austrian neurologist, who founded the practice of psychoanalysis. Relatively early in his career, Freud studied with Charcot and adopted some of his methods before concluding that encouraging patients to talk freely was a more effective treatment for neuroses or hysteria than hypnosis. In 1895, Freud co-authored *Studies on Hysteria* where he suggested that repressed, upsetting memories were at the root of hysterical symptoms. It is perhaps this study that Tess has in mind when arguing with Dr Maudsley in his lecture (p. 33).

GALILEO GALILEI (1564–1642)

Galileo was one of the first scientists to develop a telescope that was capable of observing the heavens. Through one, he made the first recorded observations of the phases of Venus, which furthered the theory of Copernican heliocentrism. However, it brought him into conflict with the dominant religious orthodoxy, culminating in his trial and condemnation by the Roman Catholic Inquisition for his support of heliocentrism. Maeve attributes Galileo's discoveries, like those of Copernicus, to his ability to dream of something bigger than that which is in front of him (p. 55).

HIPPOCRATES (*c.* 460 BC–*c.* 370 BC)

Ancient Greek physician, who argued that diseases were caused naturally rather than being inflicted by the gods. Even though many of his findings have since been disproved, many remain valid and he greatly influenced medicine for centuries to come (including lending his name to the Hippocratic Oath). A treatise in a collection of writings based on Hippocrates's work suggested that the uterus moves around the body, which Dr Maudsley and Holmes debate in his lecture (p. 30).

IMMANUEL KANT (1724–1804)

German philosopher, who greatly contributed to the discipline of deontological ethics – the idea that the rightness or wrongness of an action can be based on a set of rules. He argued that a categorical imperative is a principle that is intrinsically good and must be obeyed in all situations and circumstances if people are to observe moral laws. Miss Blake sets the women the task of contrasting Kant's theory with the Pluralistic Deontology of another thinker, W.D. Ross, who argued that there are seven duties that need to be taken into consideration when deciding what to do (p. 26).

JOHN KEATS (1795–1821)

One of the foremost Romantic poets, who, despite dying young, had become a renowned figure by the late-Victorian period, and who Tess cannot read without thinking of Ralph (p. 102).

JOHANNES KEPLER (1571–1630)

German mathematician and astronomer whose laws of planetary motion furthered Copernican heliocentrism and established that planets move in elliptical orbits around the sun. Kepler's work combined science with his own religious principles. He combined study of the convergence of Jupiter and Saturn and the appearance of a supernova with a mathematical calculation determining the birth of Christ to theorise on the Star of Bethlehem – a theme picked up in Tess's work. During his career, Kepler also served as the imperial mathematician to the Holy Roman Emperor and developed a design for a refracting telescope.

JEAN-BAPTISTE LAMARCK (1744–1829)

French naturalist, who developed a theory of evolution stating that characteristics developed over an organism's life are passed on to their offspring. In her viva, Tess is questioned about Cuvier's critique of Lamarck's theory (p. 106).

LAO TSU (c. 600 BC)

Ancient Chinese philosopher, considered the founder of Taoism and (according to legend) the author of its central text the

Tao Te Ching, although his actual historical existence is disputed. Throughout the nineteenth century, trade and treaties opened up Chinese ports to the British, yet it would still be remarkable to the other women that Carolyn should be able to quote a monk that she met while in Shanghai (p. 24).

PIERRE-MARC-GASTON DE LÉVIS (1764–1830)

French politician, who Maeve correctly identifies as being responsible for the aphorism 'Judge a man by his questions not by his answers' in Mr Banks's class (p. 17).

CHRISTOPHER MARLOWE (1564–1593)

Leading Elizabethan playwright responsible for plays such as *Tamburlaine the Great*, *The Jew of Malta*, *Edward II* and *Doctor Faustus*. Marlowe studied at Corpus Christi College, Cambridge and is one of the figures that Lloyd mentions when criticising the women's attendance at the university (p. 89).

JOHN MILTON (1608–1674)

English poet, notably of *Paradise Lost*, who studied at Christ's College, Cambridge, and is listed by Lloyd (p. 88).

THOMAS MOORE (1779–1852)

Irish poet whose work 'The Last Rose of Summer', sung by Edwards to the surprise of his fellow students (p. 95), was set to a traditional folk tune and formed part of his collection of Irish melodies. Those were published in the first half of the nineteenth century, although throughout the Victorian era other composers developed their own arrangements for the piece. Although famed as a poet, and having sung and composed for Queen Victoria, Moore initially studied law and travelled to Europe, Bermuda and North America in his lifetime.

NAPOLEON BONAPARTE (1769–1821)

French military leader who conquered a large empire across Europe, and who Carolyn incorrectly offers as an answer during Mr Banks's class (p. 17).

ISAAC NEWTON (1643–1727)

Newton is one of the most influential scientists of all time and his three laws of motion form the basis of Mr Banks's first class with the Girton students (p. 20). He allegedly developed his theory of gravitational force when an apple fell on his head as he sat under a tree – the origin of a joke shared by the women in Miss Blake's class (p. 25). Newton studied at Trinity College, Cambridge, and is mentioned by Lloyd (p. 89).

WILLIAM PITT (1759–1806)

Known as 'Pitt the Younger' (to differentiate him from his father, who also served as Prime Minister). In 1783, Pitt became the youngest Prime Minister at the age of twenty-four, having attended Pembroke College, Cambridge, from his teens – as mentioned by Lloyd (p. 89).

PLATO (c. 427 BC–c. 347 BC)

Ancient Greek philosopher who founded the Academy (an institution of higher learning) in Athens. His writings, including *The Republic*, have formed the basis of Western political philosophy, and the fact that Lloyd says he knew Plato's teachings by the age of seven shows the extent of his education (p. 88).

JEAN-JACQUES ROUSSEAU (1712–1778)

Philosopher whose work greatly influenced the Jacobins during the French Revolution, and who is incorrectly cited by Celia in Mr Banks's class (p. 17).

THOMAS SHADWELL (*c.* 1642–1692)

English poet laureate who studied at Gonville and Caius College, Cambridge, and is mentioned by Lloyd, who fails to acknowledge that Shadwell actually left the college without a degree (p. 89).

WILLIAM SHAKESPEARE (1564–1616)

The most renowned playwright in the English language, Shakespeare and his works are referenced throughout *Blue Stockings*. In his first class with the women, Mr Banks deliberately misattributes a quotation to Shakespeare's *The Taming of the Shrew*, a play in which a strong-willed woman is abused and thus apparently tamed by her husband. Tess correctly observes that the line is in fact spoken by Touchstone, the jester, in *As You Like It*, which portrays women in a quite different light. With its heroine Rosalind, disguised as a man, fleeing her uncle's tyranny and finding love in the Forest of Arden, *As You Like It* is a much more resonant play for the women in their bloomers, riding their bicycles to freedom in their college set apart from the rest of Cambridge. Later, in Miss Blake's class, Tess quotes from Shakespeare's *Henry VI Part 2* – an indication of her love of poetry, even before Ralph is on the scene.

SOCRATES (*c.* 470 BC–*c.* 399 BC)

Ancient Greek philosopher, whose teachings are primarily understood through the writings of his student, Plato. In her classes, Miss Blake employs the Socratic method by asking the women questions to stimulate their critical thought and draw out contradictions in their positions on a topic, leading them to form stronger hypotheses.

VINCENT VAN GOGH (1853–1890)

Prolific Dutch painter, notable for his bold use of colour, whose fame grew after his suicide. The post-impressionist (a term not coined until the early 1900s) movement to which van Gogh belonged was a reaction against the naturalistic depiction of light and colour, and Maeve argues that van Gogh approached his art like a science (p. 55).

JOHANNES VERMEER (1632–1675)

Renowned for his use of light and pigment, Dutch artist Vermeer is known for his depictions of domestic scenes, usually featuring women. There are therefore echoes of Vermeer's subjects in Tess's description of the girl she knows from home, Annabel, who she mentions before confessing that she cannot help but think of Ralph when she looks at Vermeer's works (p. 102).

QUEEN VICTORIA (1819–1901)

Having inherited the throne at the age of eighteen, Queen Victoria reigned as a constitutional monarch for sixty-three years, during which time her reputation and popularity faced many challenges. She married Prince Albert of Saxe-Coburg and Gotha in 1840 and they had nine children before his death at the age of forty-two in 1861. After his death, Victoria withdrew considerably from public life and wore mourning dress for the next forty year, prompting comments about her dress sense from Tess and Carolyn (p. 24).

ROBERT WALPOLE (1676–1745)

British statesman who rose to power and led the House of Commons during the South Sea Bubble financial crisis. Having been appointed First Lord of the Treasury in 1721, Walpole is held to be the first and longest serving Prime Minister. He studied at Eton and then King's College, Cambridge, and is mentioned by Lloyd in his list of notable alumni (p. 89).

Endnotes

1.   'On the Programme of the Women's Franchise League. An Address Delivered at The National Liberal Club, Feb. 25, 1890, by Mrs F. Fenwick Miller.'

2.   Emmeline Pankhurst (1858–1928) was involved in the suffrage movement from her teenage years. Along with her husband, she initially founded the Women's Franchise League, which campaigned for the rights of married women to vote in local elections. After his death she established the WSPU, which was later led by her daughter Christabel. The WSPU was committed to achieving suffrage through 'deeds not words' and, like many other women, Pankhurst was arrested on numerous occasions, went on hunger strike and was force-fed. With the outbreak of war in 1914, the suffragettes (unlike Fawcett's NUWSS) turned their energies to supporting the war effort.

3.   Emily Davies, *The Higher Education of Women* (London and New York: Alexander Strahan, 1866), p. 59.

4.   Emily Davies (1830–1921) was a committed proponent of the education of women, as well as women's suffrage, and later served as Girton's mistress and secretary. Davies was a founding member of the women's discussion group the Kensington Society and a member of the NUWSS, as she opposed the violent tactics used by the suffragettes.

5.   Alfred Waterhouse (1830–1905) was an English architect associated with the Gothic Revival (an architectural school inspired by medieval Gothic architecture that became hugely popular in the nineteenth century). Alongside a number of Oxford and Cambridge colleges, his notable works include Manchester Town Hall and the Natural History Museum in London.

6.   Jane Robinson, *Bluestockings: The Remarkable Story of the First Women to Fight for an Education* (London: Penguin, 2010), pp. 46–7.

7. *Ibid.*, p. 115.

8. Mary Ellen Waithe and Samantha Cicero, 'E. E. Constance Jones (1848–1922)', in *A History of Women Philosophers, 1900–Today*, Volume 4, ed. M. E. Waithe (Dordrecht: Kluwer Academic Publishers, 1995), pp. 25–46.

9. Jessica Swale, *Blue Stockings* (London: Nick Hern Books, 2014), p. 102. [All subsequent page references are to this edition, and are indicated in the text.]

10. See Susan M. Parkes, 'Irish Women at Cambridge, 1875–1904', in *Knowing Their Place? The Intellectual Life of Women in the 19th Century*, ed. Brendan Walsh (Dublin: The History Press Ireland, 2013).

11. Henry Maudsley, 'Sex in Mind and in Education', *Popular Science Monthly*, Volume 5 (June 1874).

12. Dante's sonnet has all the tropes of a romantic piece of lyricism: the universals, the physical love, the passion. It opens with the poet asking his friends to help him to understand a dream in which he is given a garland by a beautiful woman. Ralph stops reciting the poem just after the dreamer recounts embracing the woman tenderly, and before he talks of kissing her. The sonnet inspired numerous poetic responses from Dante's contemporaries, which further highlights the idea of Tess and Ralph being a meeting of minds, and is reflected in her attempt to write Ralph her own poem in Act Two, Scene Five.

13. See Mike Alfreds, *Different Every Night* (London: Nick Hern Books, 2009), pp. 178–82.

14. The cancan is a fast-paced and physically demanding dance, usually performed by female dancers (but occasionally by men), involving high kicks, cartwheels and other types of splits. From its origins in nineteenth-century France, the cancan had erotic connotations stemming from the way the dancers lifted their skirts to reveal their stockings, and the establishments where it was performed, such as Paris's Moulin Rouge. Moreover, at the time women wore bloomers with an open crotch, so their high kicks might even have afforded men a view of what was underneath!

15.   Although the play does not specify exactly where they meet, perhaps it is at Castle Hill, which is almost midway between Girton and Trinity colleges and therefore a suitable meeting point for the couple.

16.   Robert Carroll and Stephen Prickett (eds.), *The Bible: Authorized King James Version* (Oxford and New York: Oxford University Press, 2008), p. 776.

17.   In English folklore, Maid Marian is Robin Hood's love interest and is usually depicted as a rebellious, tomboy-ish figure. Perhaps one of Jane Austen's best-known protagonists, Elizabeth Bennet is the heroine of *Pride and Prejudice* (published 1813) who is determined to marry for love, rather than social prestige or financial expediency. In Austen's *Sense and Sensibility* (published 1811), young Marianne falls for the dashing but unreliable Willoughby and is a contrast to her older, sensible sister.

18.   The amended title of Charles Astor Bristed's *Five Years in an English University*, which talks about his experience at Cambridge in the 1840s and 1850s.

19.   Virginia Woolf's *A Room of One's Own* is an extended essay, first published in 1929, that was based on lectures the author delivered at Newnham College and Girton College in Cambridge in the preceding year. In it, Woolf charts a history of female authorship and the limitations that have been put on them, arguing that women need financial and personal independence in order to write.

20.   Virginia Woolf, *A Room of One's Own* (London: Penguin, 2000), p. 76.

21.   William Blake (1757–1827) was a Romantic poet and painter, whose work is deeply symbolic and influenced a wide range of nineteenth-century artists and composers.

22.   Edward Elgar (1857–1934) was an English composer who rose to fame in the late 1890s with his 'Enigma Variations' – an orchestral work comprising fourteen variations on an original theme, with each variation based on one of Elgar's acquaintances. Austrian Gustav Mahler (1860–1911) established himself in his lifetime as a leading conductor, but after his death his symphonic compositions, notably his

Second Symphony, known as the 'Resurrection Symphony' with its first movement representing a funeral march, cemented his reputation.

23. Steve Reich (b. 1936) is an American composer at the forefront of minimalism, which in a musical context refers to work employing limited resources, be those physical (such as instruments) or audible (such as notes). Such work tends to be characterised by repetition, sustained notes or chords (drones) and, as in some of Reich's compositions, the experimental foregrounding of the process through which sounds are made.

24. Scott Joplin (c. 1867–1917) was an African American composer who wrote numerous ragtime pieces, a genre characterised by syncopated rhythms that grew in fame throughout the 1890s. With recorded music in its infancy, ragtime pieces were often publicised and distributed as sheet music.

25. George Butterworth (1885–1916) and Ralph Vaughan Williams (1872–1958) were composers and acquaintances who were both heavily influenced by English folk traditions. They collected folk melodies, which they then based their own compositions on (such as Butterworth's 'The Banks of Green Willow'), and wrote pieces based on others' poetry, often itself inspired by nature. Likewise, authors J. R. R. Tolkien (1892–1973) and C. S. Lewis (1898–1963) were also close acquaintances; both are well-known for their fantasy novels for children (*The Hobbit* and *The Chronicles of Narnia* books respectively) and for exploring religious themes in their writing.

26. Josephine March is the principal character in Louise May Alcott's *Little Women*, which was published in 1868–9. Jo is a wilful woman who loves literature and pursues a career as a writer in New York. She initially rejects the idea of marrying (and turns down her best friend from home, Laurie), before ultimately deciding to marry a German professor.

27. Elliot Forbes (ed.) *Thayer's Life of Beethoven* (Princeton, New Jersey: Princeton University Press, 1967), p. 494.

PAGE TO STAGE

Written by established theatre professionals, the volumes in the *Page to Stage* series offer highly accessible guides to the world's best-known plays – from an essentially theatrical perspective.

Unlike fiction and poetry, the natural habitat of the play is not the printed page but the living stage. It is therefore often difficult, when reading a play on the page, to grasp how much the staging can release and enhance its true meaning.

The purpose of this series, *Page to Stage*, is to bring this theatrical perspective into the picture – and apply it to some of the best-known, most performed and most studied plays in our literature. Moreover, the authors of these guides are not only well-known theatre practitioners but also established writers, giving them an unrivalled insight and authority.

TITLES IN THE PAGE TO STAGE SERIES

Chekhov's Three Sisters
Michael Pennington

Ibsen's A Doll's House
Stephen Unwin

Timberlake Wertenbaker's Our Country's Good
Max Stafford-Clark with Maeve McKeown

Diane Samuels' Kindertransport
Diane Samuels

Jessica Swale's Blue Stockings
Jessica Swale and Lois Jeary